The Book Of Acts

Chapter Summary Notes

Dr. Phil Fernandes

Introduction to Acts

Author – Luke (colleague of Paul)

Date – around 61 AD (ends abruptly, before deaths of James, Peter, & Paul)

Readers – Theophilus

Purpose & Theme - (Acts 1:1-3)
-the sequel to Luke (history of early church)
-many convincing proofs of resurrection

Outline #1 (Acts 1:8)
A) Christianity spreads in Jerusalem
B) Christianity spreads in Palestine & Syria
C) Christianity spreads throughout ancient world

Outline #2
A) the acts of Peter (chapters 1-12)
B) the acts of Paul (chapters 13-28)

Acts One

Many Convincing Proofs (vs 1-4)

The Promise of the Holy Spirit (4-8)
    -He will empower the apostles to be His
      witnesses

Jesus Ascends to Heaven (9-11)

List of the Apostles (12-14)

Replacing Judas (15-26)
    -Matthias replaces Judas
    -Judas' death (he hung himself, body fell)

Acts Two

The Holy Spirit Baptizes the Church (vs 1-4)

SPIRITUAL GIFTS
1 COR 13-15 12-14

The Response of the Crowd (5-13)

SOME MOCKED THEM SAYING THEY WERE DRUNK (2:13)
THE REST WERE AMAZED

Peter Defends the Actions of the Disciples as the Work of God (14-21)

1. IT'S TOO EARLY TO BE DRUNK (2:15)
2. ONLY DEFEND YOURSELF IF IT DEFENDS THE GOSPEL
3. RESPONDED WITH OLD TESTIMENT SCRIPTURE (JOEL 2:28 - 2:32)
NOTE: THE LAST DAYS STARTED WHEN JESUS CAME THE FIRST TIME.

Peter Proclaims Jesus' Resurrection (22-36)

THE CROSS WAS ALWAYS THE PLAN. RESURRECTION FULLFIELD OLD TESTIMENT PROPHECY

The Result of Peter's Sermon—3,000 saved (37-41)

REPENT & BAPTIZED (ALL THAT BELIEVED)

The First Christian Church (41-47) → ASK ?'s BOUBTS BELIEVES

- spread gospel (HOW? NO ONE WANTS TO BE PREACHED @ TODAY) - Lord's Supper
- baptize   - Holy Spirit's power
- apostles' teaching   - sharing with others (SHARE WHAT YOU OWN)
- fellowship   - praising God
- prayer

"PEOPLE OF THE BOOK"

Acts 3

Peter heals the lame man (vs 1-10) 5 4 P's
  • THESE VERSES SHOW GODS POWER, THEN PREACHING, PERSECUTION, PRAYER
                                                                    POSSESSIONS

Peter preaches to the crowd (vs 11-26)
    -he preaches the death & resurrection of Jesus
    -eyewitness testimony
    -repent & accept Jesus as Savior & Messiah
    -when Israel accepts Jesus as her Messiah, God
            will restore all things (millennium) REV: 20

Acts 4

DESPITE PERSECUTION THE EARLY CHURCH CONTINUED TO
GROW.

Peter & John are arrested (vs 1-4)
FOR HEALING + PREACHING IN JESUS NAME (PERSECUTION)

Peter & John before the Sanhedrin (5-22)
    -Pharisees = rabbis (teachers of Old Testament)
    -Sadducees = temple priests (deny resurrection)
    -we must obey God rather than men
- ACTS 4:5 - 4:12 = BOLDNESS!

The believers pray for more boldness (23-31)

The believers share their possessions (32-37)

Acts 5

Ananias & Sapphira (vs 1-11)
    -they lied to the Holy Spirit
    -God strikes them dead
    -great fear came over the whole church

Apostolic Signs & Wonders (vs 12-16)
    -healings, exorcisms, etc.
    -2 Corinthians 12:12
    -the church was united (Jesus is our unity)

The Apostles are Arrested (vs 17-42)
    -the Sadducees arrested the apostles
    -an angel frees the apostles
    -apostles preached in the temple
    -arrested again & tried by the Sanhedrin
    -"we must obey God rather than men"
    -Gamaliel intervenes
    -the apostles flogged & set free
    -the apostles rejoice

Acts 6

Choosing the 7 Deacons (vs 1-7)
    -Hellenistic Jews vs Hebrews
    -Hellenistic widows overlooked for food
     distribution
    -7 Hellenistic Jewish men chosen
    -this restored unity on the church
    -the Jerusalem church grew

Stephen is Arrested (vs 8-15)
    -one of the 7 deacons (miracles, preaching)
    -Synagogue of the Freedmen brought him to
        the Sanhedrin
    -Jesus signaled the end of the temple order

Acts 7

Stephen's Final Sermon (vs 1-53)
- charged with speaking against the temple & the Mosaic law
- main points of his sermon
    - God's presence is not restricted to any one location
    - the Jews' continued rejection of God's messengers
- outline of his sermon
    - the Jewish fathers (not in Promised Land)
    - Joseph (Israel in Egypt)
    - Moses & wilderness wandering
    - Tabernacle & Temple-God's presence is not restricted to one location
    - the temple is not essential to true worship
    - Jesus is the true temple (incarnation)
    - Jesus accuses his persecutors of killing the Messiah
- the death of Stephen
- Saul (Paul) approved of their actions

Acts 8

Saul persecutes the Church (vs 1-3)
    -house to house searches
    -primarily directed at Hellenistic Jewish
        believers (considered anti-temple)
    -Christians fled & were scattered throughout
        Judea & Samaria
    -the apostles did not have to flee
    -Jerusalem church became primarily Hebrew

The scattered believers spread the Gospel (4)

Philip preaches the Gospel in Samaria (4-8)
    -one of the 7 deacons (most wanted list)
    -Philip preached Jesus, performed miracles
    -entire multitude accepted Christ

Simon the Sorcerer (secret, occultic, magic)
    -professed faith in Christ (9-13)

Peter & John investigate the situation (14-17)
    -one Church (Jew, Smaritan, Gentile)
    -baptized new converts with the Holy Spirit
    1 CORINTHIANS 12
    LUKE 11 9-13 (ASK, SEEK, KNOCK)

Acts 8 (continued)

Peter confronts Simon the Sorcerer (18-25)

-Simon tries to buy spiritual power from the apostles (not a true believer)

-Peter tells him his money would perish with him

-Simon feared God's judgment

-Simon Magus (founder of Gnosticism?)

-Peter & John preached throughout Samaria & returned to Jerusalem

1. EVEN IN ADVERSITY PREACH THE WORD

2. GOSPEL IS FOR ALL PEOPLE AND ALL NATIONS

3. NOT EVERYONE IS A BELIEVER WHO SAYS THEY ARE

4. TRUE BELIEVERS ARE IN CHRIST AND FILLED W/ THE HOLY SPIRIT

Philip leads Ethiopian Eunuch to Christ (26-40)

-he explains Isaiah 53 to him

-the Eunuch believes & is baptized

-the Holy Spirit snatches Philip away

-Philip continued preaching Jesus

Acts 9

Saul the Persecutor (vs 1-2)
- -he disagreed with his rabbi Gamaliel
- -he persecuted Hellenistic Jewish Christians
- -he received authority from High Priest to arrest Christians in Damascus
- -synagogues-places to worship & hear OT
- -Damascus-140 miles NE of Jerusalem
- -the Way-ancient name for Christianity

Jesus appears to Saul (3-6)
- -on the road to Damascus
- -"Why are you persecuting Me?"

Saul was blinded by the light (vs 7-9)
- -led by the hand to Damascus
- -blind for 3 days; didn't eat or drink

God commands Ananias to heal Saul (10-16)
- -Ananias was a disciple living in Damascus
- -the Lord appeared to him in a vision
- -he was reluctant to heal Paul (fear; anger)
- -Saul will be the apostle to the Gentiles
- -Saul will suffer greatly for Christ

Ananias Heals & Baptizes Saul (17-19)

Saul preaches in Damascus synagogues (20-22)
    -the power of Jesus to change lives
    -Paul's message = Jesus is Messiah & Son
        of God
    -Paul refuted Jews in debate

Saul escapes Damascus (23-25)
    -rescued by believers
    -had preached in Damascus for 3 years
        (Gal 1:15-18)

Saul preaches in Jerusalem (26-29)
    -the disciples were afraid of him
    -Barnabas came to his side
    -Saul preached to the Hellenists in Jerusalem
    -he picked up where Stephen left off

Saul rescued again & sent to Tarsus (30)

The church enjoys peace & growth (31)
    -freedom from persecution

Peter heals a paralyzed man in Lydda (32-35)

Peter raises Tabitha from the dead in Joppa (36-42)

The signs of an apostle (2 Corinthians 12:12)

Peter stayed many days in Joppa with Simon the Tanner (43)

Acts 10

Cornelius-a man seeking God (vs 1-8)
    -unsaved, but seeking God
    -centurion (led 100 Roman soldiers)
    -an angel tells him to send for Peter

Peter's Vision (vs 9-16)
    -a sheet descending from heaven
    -filled with unclean animals
    -God orders him to "kill & eat"
    -the vision is repeated 3 times
    -Old Testament dietary laws no longer in
        effect; Gentiles no longer "unclean"

Men Sent by Cornelius Find Peter (17-23)

Peter Preaches at Cornelius' House (24-43)
    -Jesus is Messiah & Lord of all
    -He was crucified, but God raised Him
        from the dead
    -forgiveness through belief in Jesus

Acts 10 (continued)

Cornelius & Household are Saved (44-48)
- -baptized by Holy Spirit (Gentiles)
- -they spoke in tongues
- -Jew & Gentile = one Church
- -Peter & friends baptize them
- -Peter & friends stay with Cornelius a
  few days

Acts 11

Peter is Criticized by Legalistic Jews (1-3)

Peter Explains His Actions (4-18)
-God led him to Cornelius
-God baptized Gentiles with the same
    Holy Spirit as the Jews
-Peter's former critics praise God for
    saving the Gentiles

The Church in Antioch/Syria Grows (19-30)
-Gentile church was growing in Antioch
-Jerusalem church sent Barnabas to
    check things out
-Barnabas went to Tarsus & got Paul
-he brought Paul to Antioch to teach
-believers first called Christians-Antioch
-Agabus-prophet predicted a famine that
    would devastate Jerusalem church
-Barnabas & Saul brought the donation
    to Jerusalem church

Acts 12

Herod Agrippa I (1-5)
-beheads James (John's brother-43AD?)
-arrests Peter (church prays for Peter)

Peter Miraculously Freed From Prison(6-18)
-God sends an angel to free Peter
-Peter (& apostles) flee Jerusalem
-Jesus' half-brother James now leads the
Jerusalem church

The Death of Herod Agrippa I (19-23)
-he accepted worship from men
-God struck him dead (44AD)

The Word of God Spreads (24)

Paul & Barnabas Return to Antioch (25)
-with John Mark
-after they completed their mission

Acts 13

The Start of Paul & Barnabas' First Missionary Journey

-Holy Spirit tells leaders of Antioch (of Syria) church to send Paul & Barnabas on mission trip (John Mark accompanies them)

-they preach on the Island of Cyprus
- -opposed by a Jewish sorcerer named Bar-Jesus (Paul curses him with blindness)
- -Governor Sergius Paulus accepts Christ
- -John Mark returns to Jerusalem

-Paul preached in a synagogue in Antioch of Pisidia (many Gentiles converts)
- -sermon-Messiah, death & resurrection, salvation through Jesus
- -Paul-opposed by Jewish leaders
- -Paul & Barnabas go to Iconium

Acts 14

Paul & Barnabas Finish Their First Missionary Journey

-<u>Paul & Barnabas preach in Iconium</u>
-many Jews & Gentiles accept Christ
-Paul & Barnabas disciple the new converts
-the city is divided; some plot to stone them

-<u>Paul & Barnabas flee to Lystra</u>
-Paul heals a man lame from birth
-the people mistake Paul & Barnabas for 2 false gods
     (Hermes & Zeus) & try to worship them
-Paul corrects them-the Creator is the one true God
-some of the Jews from Iconium & Antioch stone
     Paul & leave him for dead
-<u>Paul got up; the next day they preached in Derbe</u>
     -led many to Christ

-<u>Paul & Barnabas return to Lystra, Iconium, &
Antioch of Pisidia</u>
-they strengthen them & select elders

-<u>Paul & Barnabas return to their home church-
Antioch of Syria-ends 1st missionary journey</u>

Acts 15

The Jerusalem Council (vs 1-34)

The Issue: Should Gentile believers have to be circumcised?

Those for circumcision of Gentiles were Pharisees who became Christians

Those opposed to circumcision for Gentile believers:
- Paul & Barnabas (the apostles to the Gentiles)
- Peter (he led Cornelius to Christ)
- James (Old Testament predicts salvation of Gentiles)

The decision announced by James (vs 19-34)
- Gentile converts will not be forced to be circumcised
- they will be encouraged to refrain from:
  - eating meat sacrificed to idols
  - sexual immorality
  - drinking blood
  - eating meat of strangled animals

Paul & Barnabas Disagree About John Mark
(vs 35-41) Paul & Silas head for Asia Minor;
Barnabas & John Mark for Cyprus

Acts 16

Paul Begins His Second Missionary Journey

-Paul takes Silas with him (vs 1-5)
-they went to Derbe & then Lystra
-Timothy was a young disciple in Lystra
    -he was half Jewish (Paul had him circumcised)
    -Paul took Timothy with him on the journey
-Paul, Silas, & Timothy preach the Gospel in the
    region

-the Holy Spirit tells Paul not to go north or south,
but to go west--Paul has a vision of a man in
Macedonia (vs 6-10)

-the "we" passages (Luke was with Paul, Silas,
    & Timothy-Acts 16:10, 11, 16, etc.)

-Paul's ministry in Philippi (11-40)
    -Lydia from Thyatira (a businesswoman) accepts
        Christ & opens her home to the
        missionaries
    -Paul casts a demon out of an annoying slave girl
    -Paul & Silas are beaten & imprisoned
    -Paul & Silas sing praises at midnight in the
        Philippian jail

-an earthquake frees the prisoners
-believing the prisoners have escaped, the
     Philippian jailer prepares to kill himself
-Paul tells him that no one has escaped
-the jailer asks Paul about salvation
-Paul tells him to trust in the Lord Jesus (31)
-the jailer & his family accept Christ
-the authorities find out that they have beaten
     Roman citizens; they apologize & beg them
     to leave
-Paul & Silas return to Lydia's house

Acts 17

Paul & Silas continue the second missionary journey

-Paul preaches in synagogues of <u>Thessalonica</u> (1-9)
    -Jesus is Messiah; His death & resurrection
    -some Jews & many Gentiles get saved
    -Paul & Silas arrested but later released

-Paul preaches in <u>Berea</u> (10-15)
    -Bereans tested Paul's teachings with the Word
        of God (vs 11)
    -many Bereans come to Christ
    -Jews from Thessalonica cause a riot
    -Paul leaves for Athens

-<u>Paul preaches in Athens on Mars Hill</u> (16-34)
    -the city is filled with idols
    -Greek philosophers (Stoic & Epicurean)
    -Paul says he knows the "unknown God"
    -this God created all things
    -this God desires to save those who repent & call
        out to Him
    -this God will someday judge the world through
        Jesus Christ, whom He has raised from the
        Dead
    -the reaction of Paul's listeners (32-34)
        -mocking, not sure, believing

Acts 18

Paul leaves Athens & goes to Corinth (1-17)
  -he meets Aquila & Priscilla (tentmakers like
      him; they are from Rome)
  -Paul preaches the gospel in Corinth synagogue
      to Jews & Greeks
  -Silas & Timothy arrive in Corinth & relieve
      Paul of secular work so Paul could devote
      his time to preaching
  -Paul argued that Jesus is the Jewish Messiah
  -the Jews rejected Paul's message
  -Paul went to the Gentiles
  -God encourages Paul in a vision
  -Paul stays & preaches in Corinth for 1 ½ years
  -unsaved Jews arrest Paul, but the Roman
      Governor Gallio refuses to try Paul
  -Crispus (the synagogue leader) & many others
      in Corinth are saved

Paul in Cenchrea (18)
  -Paul takes a Nazarite vow

Paul in Ephesus (19-21)
  -Paul preached in the synagogue
  -he departs, but leaves Aquila & Priscilla to
      minister

Acts 18 (continued)

Paul completes the 2nd missionary journey (22)
    -he returns to Antioch of Syria (his home church)

Paul begins his 3rd missionary journey (23)
    -he strengthened the disciples in Galatia &
        Phrygia

Apollos (24-28)
    -he was a powerful preacher & teacher from
        Alexandria, Egypt (well educated)
    -he was Jewish, but believed Jesus was the
        Messiah
    -he only knew the baptism of John
    -Aquila & Priscilla invited him to their home &
        explained the ways of God to him more
        thoroughly (doctrine of Holy Spirit?)
    -he came to Ephesus & vigorously refuted the
        Jews in the synagogues in public debate
    -Apollos went to Achaia & argued from
        Scripture that Jesus is the Jewish Messiah
    -he became a great leader in the early church

Acts 19

Paul Continues His 3rd Missionary Journey

-Paul leaves Galatia & goes to Ephesus
    -at this time Apollos was at Corinth
    -Paul found 12 disciples at Ephesus (1-7)
        -they never heard of the Holy Spirit
        -they only knew John's baptism
        -Paul told them about Jesus & baptized them
        -they spoke in tongues & prophesied
    -first 3 months in Ephesus-Paul preached in the
        synagogues (8)
    -final 2 years-due to hostility Paul preached in
        the school of Tyrannus in Ephesus (9-10)
    -God heals people through Paul's cloths (11-12)
    -the 7 sons of Sceva are severely beaten by a
        demon-possessed man (13-17)
    -Paul leads many occultists to Christ; they burn
        their books (18-20)
    -Paul promises to visit Rome in future (21-22)
    -worshippers of the goddess Artemis led by
        Demetrius (a shrine maker) nearly
        cause a riot (23-34)
    -the city official disperses the crowd telling them
        to handle the situation through the courts
        (35-41)

Acts 20

Paul Continues His 3rd Missionary Journey

Paul in Macedonia & Greece (1-6)

-he spends 3 months there
-the Jews plot to take his life
-Paul & 7 others go to Troas

Paul in Troas (7-12)

-Paul preached until midnight
-a young man named Eutychus accidentally falls to his death from an upper window
-Paul raises him from the dead

-Paul rushes to Miletus en route to Jerusalem for the Feast of Pentecost (13-16)

-In Miletus, Paul gives his farewell message to the Ephesian elders (17-38)

-Paul reminds them of his uncompromising ministry
-this will be their final meeting
-Paul tells them to feed & shepherd God's flock
-he warns them to watch for false teachers who will enter the church (wolves)
-Paul prays for the Ephesian elders
-they wept, embraced Paul, & went with him to the ship

Acts 21

-<u>Paul en route to Tyre</u> (1-3)
-Paul stays a week in Tyre (4-6)
    -the disciples urged him not to go to Jerusalem
    -Paul stops in Ptolemais for one day (7)
-<u>Paul in Caesarea</u> (8-15)
    -Paul visits Philip (one of the 7 deacons)
    -Philip has 4 unmarried daughters who prophesy
    -the prophet Agabus warns Paul that he will be
        imprisoned in Jerusalem
    -the believers beg Paul not to go
    -Paul is convinced God wants him to go to
        Jerusalem
-<u>Paul in Jerusalem</u> (16-40)
    -Paul reports to James & the Jerusalem elders
        about his ministry to the Gentiles
    -Paul is accused of opposing the Law of Moses
        & circumcision for Jewish believers
    -Paul is advised to shave his head & take a vow
        in the temple (1 Corinthians 9:19-22)
    -an angry Jewish mob attacks Paul believing he
        is against Jewish Law & that he brought a
        Gentile into the temple (they try to kill him)
    -Paul is rescued by Roman troops
    -the Roman commander mistook Paul for an
        Egyptian rebel
    -Paul gets permission to speak to the angry mob

Acts 22

-<u>Paul speaks in Aramaic to the angry crowd</u> (1-21)
    -he gives his testimony
    -he is a Jew born in Tarsus, but trained in the
        Law of Moses by Gamaliel in Jerusalem
    -he persecuted Christians
    -but he was converted when Jesus appeared to
        him on the road to Damascus
    -God sent him to preach to the Gentiles

-<u>The crowd again becomes violent</u> (22-23)
    -because Paul said he was sent to the Gentiles

-<u>Roman soldiers rescue Paul from the mob</u> (24-29)
    -the commander ordered that Paul be scourged
    -he changes his mind when Paul tells him that he
        is a Roman citizen
    -the commander was sorry he had put a Roman
        citizen in chains

-<u>Paul is taken before the Sanhedrin</u> (30)
    -the next day the Roman commander brought
        Paul before the Jewish ruling council

Acts 23

-<u>Paul appears before the Sanhedrin</u> (1-10)
  -the Jewish high Priest Ananias orders others to strike Paul
  -Paul divides the Sanhedrin
    -Paul states that he is a Pharisee & that he is on trial because he believes in the resurrection
    -the Sadducees deny the resurrection, spirits, & angels (Pharisees accept all three)
    -the Pharisees temporarily back Paul
    -a dispute erupts between the two parties
    -Roman soldiers remove Paul for his own protection

-<u>The Lord appears to & comforts Paul at night</u> (11)
  -Paul will witness for Jesus in Rome

-<u>a conspiracy to kill Paul</u> (12-22)
  -over 40 men vow not to eat or drink until they kill Paul
  -Paul's nephew hears of the plot & tells Paul & the Roman commander
-<u>470 soldiers transport Paul to Caesarea</u> (23-35)
  -the Roman commander writes a letter to Felix, governor of Caesarea, explaining why Paul is being sent to him

Acts 24

-<u>Ananias</u> (the Jewish High Priest) went to Caesarea with his colleagues to make their case against Paul before <u>Roman Governor Felix</u> (vs 1-9)

-<u>their charges</u>—Paul causes riots among the Jews worldwide, he tried to desecrate the temple, & he is a leader of the Nazarene sect

-Paul denied that he causes riots & tried to desecrate the temple, but he admits he is a follower of the Way (10-21)

-<u>Governor Felix</u> did not want to offend the High Priest so he promised to decide the case at a later time; he kept Paul under guard but with freedom to have guests (22-23)

-Paul preached to Felix & his wife Drusilla during a private meeting, but Felix dismisses Paul due to his fear of future judgment (24-25)

-For the next 2 years Felix visits Paul hoping to receive a bribe from him for his release; of course, Paul does not comply (26-27)

Acts 25

-<u>Festus</u> replaces Felix as Governor

-Jewish leaders ask Festus to bring Paul to Jerusalem,
      for they are plotting to kill him (1-3)
-Festus refuses—Paul will remain in Caesarea for his
      trial (4-5)
-the Jewish leaders go to Caesarea to bring charges
      against Paul, but they fail to prove them (6-7)
-Paul pleads innocent, refuses to be tried in
      Jerusalem, & appeals his case to Caesar (8-12)

-<u>King Herod Agrippa II</u> visits Governor Festus (13)

-Festus tells Agrippa about Paul's case (14-21)
      -a religious dispute about a dead man named
            Jesus whom Paul claims is alive (vs 19)
-King Agrippa requests to meet with Paul (22)
-the next day King Agrippa & his sister Bernice are
      introduced to Paul (23-27)

Acts 26

Paul Speaks to King Herod Agrippa II

-Paul shares his personal testimony (vs 1-23)
    -he was a Pharisee who strictly obeyed God's
        Laws
    -he persecuted Christians
    -Jesus confronted him on the road to Damascus
    -Paul accepts Jesus as Messiah & Savior
    -God appointed him to preach to the Gentiles
    -he continued to preach Jesus despite horrible
        persecution

-Governor Festus accuses Paul of being insane (24)
-Paul responds by saying that what he is saying is
    true & reasonable (25)
-Paul asks Agrippa if he believes in the prophets
    (26-27)
-Agrippa asks Paul if he really thinks he will convert
    Agrippa so quickly (28)
-Paul expresses his desire that everyone in the room
    be saved like him, though without the chains
    (29)

-after the meeting both Agrippa & Festus agree that
    Paul would have been set free if he had not
    appealed his case to Caesar/Rome (30-32)

Acts 27

Paul is shipwrecked en route to Rome

-the trip from Caesarea to Sidon (1-3)
- -Julius the centurion is placed in charge of Paul & other prisoners
- -Julius allows Paul to visit with friends

-from Sidon to Myra (4-6)
- -prisoners are transferred to an Egyptian ship headed for Italy

-from Myra to Fair Havens (7-12)
- -Paul warns the centurion not to continue the voyage due to the Mediterranean storm season
- -Paul's warning goes unheeded

-from Fair Havens to Malta (13-20)
- -a horrible storm overtakes the ship

-Paul encourages the passengers (21-38)
- -God told Paul they would be shipwrecked on an island, but that none would lose his life

-the shipwreck (39-44)
- -the ship runs aground
- -the soldiers want to kill the prisoners, thinking they might escape
- -the commanding officer forbids it in order to save Paul's life
- -everyone on board makes it safely to shore

Acts 28

-<u>Paul on the Island of Malta</u> (1-10)
    -Paul is shipwrecked on the Island on Malta
    -Paul is bitten by a poisonous snake
    -the islanders think he must have been a
        murderer
    -when Paul does not get sick from the snake bite,
        the islanders conclude that Paul must be a god
    -Paul heals the governor Publius' father from
        fever & dysentery
    -Paul begins to heal other sick islanders who
        come to him

-<u>Paul is en route to Rome</u> (11-14)
    -the ship makes 3 brief stops along the way
-<u>Paul in Rome</u> (15-31)
    -Paul is greeted by Christians in Rome
    -Paul is permitted to live by himself with a
        soldier to guard him (he is allowed visitors)
    -Paul has 2 meetings with Jewish leaders from
        Rome (he preaches the gospel to them)
    -some believe; some do not
    -Paul reminds them that their disbelief was
        predicted in the Old Testament (Isa 6:9-10)
    -for the next 2 years, Paul stays in the rented
        house, under Roman guard, & he witnesses
        to all who visit him

The Book of Acts

Instructor: Phil Fernandes, Ph.D.

Institute of Biblical Defense
P. O. Box 3264, Bremerton, WA. 98310
(360) 698-7382

www.biblicaldefense.org

ibd@sinclair.net

Introduction to Acts

1) <u>Author</u>—Luke
    A) the "we" passages of Acts (a co-laborer with Paul)
    B) all other known colleagues of Paul are mentioned
    C) addressed to Theophilus as was the Gospel of Luke
    D) use of medical terms (Luke was a physician)
    E) early church considered Luke the author of both Acts & Luke

2) <u>Date</u>—around 61AD
    A) doesn't mention the matyrdoms of Peter & Paul (67AD)
    B) doesn't mention Nero's burning of Rome (64AD)
    C) doesn't mention the destruction of the temple (70AD)
    D) Acts abruptly ends with Paul's arrival in Rome (61AD)
    E) Sir William Ramsey, one of the greatest archaeologists who
    ever lived, concluded from his research that Luke was
    one of the greatest historians of the ancient world

3) <u>Readers</u>—this letter was written to Theophilus
    A) as was the Gospel of Luke
    B) it was widely read in the ealy church
    C) it became the authoritative history of early Christianity

4) <u>Purpose & Theme</u>
    A) the history of the early church from the ascension &
        Pentecost to Paul's arrival in Rome (30-61AD)
    B) Acts shows the important transition from Jewish
        Christianity to Gentile Christianity

5) <u>Outline #1</u> (Acts 1:8)
    A) the spread of Christianity in Jerusalem (1:1-8:3)
    B) spread of Christianity in Palestine & Syria (8:4-12:25)
    C) spread of Christianity throughout the world (13:1-28:31)

6) <u>Outline #2</u>
    A) <u>the acts of Peter</u> (chapters 1-12)
        1) focuses on Peter's ministry
        2) includes Pentecost, persecution, preaching
        3) includes John & James (sons of Zebedee)
        4) includes Stephen's death, Philip's ministry
        5) includes Paul's conversion & Cornelius' conversion
    B) <u>the acts of Paul</u> (chapters 13-28)
        1) includes Paul's 3 missionary journeys
        2) includes the Jerusalem council headed by James
        3) includes Paul's arrest & journey to Rome
        4) includes Barnabas, Silas, John Mark, Timothy

Many Convincing Proofs (Acts 1:1-3)

1) this work is addressed to Theophilus
  A) as was the Gospel of Luke (Luke 1:1-4)
  B) most excellent = Theophilus may have been a Roman official
2) Luke describes his gospel as the first account written to
  Theophilus (Acts is the sequel to Luke)
3) Jesus gave strong evidence for His bodily resurrection
  A) by appearing to His disciples after His resurrection
  B) over a period of 40 days
    1) 1 Cor 15:3-8; Mt 28; Mk 16; Lk 24; Jn 20 &21
    2) 1 Jn 1:1-3; 2 Pt 1:16
4) our faith is not a blind, irrational faith
5) our faith is based upon strong evidence (history, reason, science)
6) Christianity can & should be intelligently defended
  —1 Pt 3:15; Col 4:5-6; Jude 3; Jn 20:30-31
7) Jesus spent His last 40 days on earth teaching His disciples about the
  Kingdom of God (the church, millennium, true spirituality)

The Promise of the Holy Spirit (Acts 1:4-8)

1) Jesus commanded the apostles to remain in Jerusalem (4-5)
  A) to wait for the Father's promise to be fulfilled
  B) the promise = the baptism of the Holy Spirit
  C) baptism = immersion, identification, cleansing,
    empowerment (1 Cor 12:13)
  D) water baptism symbolizes salvation & Spirit baptism
  E) John's baptism was for repentance
  F) Spirit baptism now occurs at regeneration (1 Pt 3:21)
  G) Acts covers a transitional period of time
  H) the apostles were Galileans

2) apostles ask Jesus when Kingdom will be restored to Israel (6-8)
  A) the apostles did not have a need to know the time (Mt 24:36)
  B) what they needed to know was this: (Lk 24:49)
    1) the promised Holy Spirit would come (Mt 3:11-12;
      Jn 7:37-39; 14:16-17, 26; 15:26-27; 16:7, 13-15)
    2) Joel 2:28; Isa 32:15; 44:3; Ezk 39:28-29; Zech 12:10
    3) Holy Spirit will empower the apostles & the church
      —spiritual power, not political power
    4) they shall be Christ's witnesses
      a) Jerusalem (city)
      b) Judea & Samaria (region)
      c) to the remotest part of the earth (world)

Jesus Ascends into Heaven (Acts 1:9-11)

1) after this, Jesus bodily ascended into heaven (9)
      —Mount of Olives (Ac 1:12; Mt 24; Zech 14:4)
2) two angels instruct the apostles (10-11)
      A) don't get distressed by Jesus' departure
      B) have courage—He will return
      C) this same Jesus will return
            —refutes Moon, Bahai Faith, New Age, etc.
      D) He will return in the same way in which He left
          A) bodily, visible, clouds, miraculous
          B) Rv 1:7; Mt 24:23-31
          C) refutes Moon, Bahai Faith, New Age, Jehovah's
          Witnesses, etc.
3) Jesus' present ministry (Psalm 110:1)
      A) Hb 4:14; 7:25; Rm 8:33-34 (He intercedes for us)
      B) Jn 12:32-33 (He draws all men to Himself)
      C) 1 John 2:1-2 (He defends believers before the Father)

The List of the Apostles (Acts 1:12-14)

1) Jesus had ascended from the Mount of Olives (Mt 24; Zech 14) {12}
2) this mount is just outside of Jerusalem (outside the eastern gate)
3) a Sabbath day's journey = about 3,000 feet
      —a Jewish legalistic tradition based on Ex 16:29 & Nm 35:5
4) the upper room {13}
      A) the Last Supper (Lk 22:12; Mk 14:15)
      B) post-resurrection appearances? (Lk 24: Jn 20)
5) lists of the apostles
    (Acts 1:13; Mt 10:2-4; Mk 3:16-19; Lk 6:14-16)

A) Peter	E) Philip	I) James, son of Alphaeus
B) John	F) Thomas	J) Simon the Zealot
C) James	G) Bartholomew	K) Judas/Thaddeus
D) Andrew	H) Matthew/Levi	L) (x—Judas Iscariot)

6) the spiritual state of the early church {14}
      A) with one mind (unity)
      B) continually devoted themselves to prayer
      C) waiting on the Lord (Ac 1:4)
      D) these 3 ingredients are necessary for a church to be used of
      God in a powerful way
7) other members of the early church with the apostles
      A) the women (Lk 8:1-3; Jn 19:25; Mt 27:55-56; 28:1)
      B) Mary, the mother of Jesus & Jesus' half-brothers (Mt 13:55;
      Mk 3:31-35; Jn 7:1-5; 1 Cor 15:3-8; Jm; Jude)

Finding a Replacement for Judas (Acts 1:15-26)

1) <u>Peter</u>—leader of the early church (Mt 16:13-20) {15}
    A) he was not infallible (Gal 2:11-14)
    B) he led Jerusalem Church until he fled persecution
    C) he probably led the church wherever he was located
2) about <u>120 believers</u> in Jerusalem (500 in Galilee?—1 Cor 15:6)
3) <u>brothers</u> = believers are a spiritual family {16-17}
4) <u>Old Testament predicted that Judas would be replaced</u>
    A) Holy Spirit spoke through David
    B) inspiration = God guided human authors to record His
        written Word without error
    C) Judas had betrayed Christ
    D) the need for a replacement (Mt 19:28)
    E) James (John's brother) was not replaced (Ac 12:1-2)
5) Luke adds information to Peter's speech {18-19}
    A) betrayal money bought a field ("the field of blood")
    B) Judas' body fell & ruptured (after death by hanging)
    C) Mt 27:3-10; Zech 11:12-13
6) Peter quotes Psalms to prove Judas must be replaced {20}
    A) Ps 69:25; 109:8
    B) see also Ps 41:9 (Jn 13:18; 17:12)
7) Peter lists <u>the qualifications</u> to be one of the 12 apostles {21-22}
    A) they must have followed Jesus from John's baptism until
    the ascension
    B) must be a witness of at least one of His post-resurrection
    appearances
8) <u>the 2 candidates for replacing Judas</u> {23}
    A) Joseph (called Barsabbas—Son of Sabbath; surnamed Justus)
    B) Matthais (Eusebius says that he was one of the 70
        disciples; Lk 10:1)
9) the apostles pray for the Lord to intervene & choose Judas'
    replacement {24-25}
10) the apostles drew lots & <u>Matthais is chosen</u> {26}
    A) Paul was appointed by Jesus to be the apostle to the
        Gentiles (Gal 1:1; 2:7)
    B) the apostles depended on God for the decision (Prov 16:33)
    C) human wisdom could narrow the choice to 2 godly men
    D) but, human wisdom was unable to choose between them
    E) Divine wisdom was needed
    F) similar to praying & then flipping a coin to decide when
    human wisdom has reached its limit

The Holy Spirit Baptizes the Church (Ac 2:1-4)

1) Introduction
>A) the 120 disciples wait on the Lord
>B) they were in prayer; they were united
>C) they were waiting for Jesus' promise of the Holy Spirit to be fulfilled (Acts 1:4-5, 8; Jn 14, 15, 16)

2) The Day of Pentecost (vs 1)
>A) the 7 Jewish Feasts
>>1) Passover (in April)
>>>a) Egypt—10th plague/death of first-born/lamb
>>>b) symbolized Christ's death (Jn 1:29; 1 Cor 5:7)
>>2) Unleavened Bread
>>>a) Israel separated from the nations
>>>b) the believer's separation (1 Cor 5:7)
>>3) First Fruits
>>>a) harvest in the land (first fruits given to Lord)
>>>b) Christ's resurrection (1 Cor 15:20-23)
>>4) Pentecost (50 days after First Fruits)
>>>a) completion of the harvest
>>>b) start of the Church (Acts 2)
>>5) Trumpets (Rosh Hashana) {Rev 11:15}
>>>a) Israel's new year (in September or October)
>>>b) tribulation, Christ's return, Israel's gathering
>>6) Day of Atonement (Yom Kippur)
>>>a) sacrifice for Israel's national sin/Holy of Holies
>>>b) Christ's return, national conversion of Israel
>>>c) Rom 11:25-27; Dan 9:24-27
>>7) Tabernacles
>>>a) Israel in the wilderness in tents
>>>b) the millennium (Zech 14:16; Rev 20:4)
>B) the Jews added 2 more feasts
>>1) Feast of Lights (Hanukkah) (December)
>>>a) instituted by Judas Maccabeus in 164BC
>>>b) temple rededicated after desecration by Antiochus Epiphanes
>>2) Feast of Purim (March)
>>>—celebrates failure of Haman's plot to wipe out the Jews (Book of Esther)
>C) required attendance for 3 annual feasts
>>1) Passover, Pentecost, Tabernacles
>>2) all healthy, obedient male Jewish adults in Jerusalem
>D) 120 believers gathered together in one place (community)

3) The Birth of the Church (vs 2-4)
    A) a noise from heaven (2)
        1) like a violent, rushing wind
        2) it filled the entire house
        3) wind is symbolic of the Holy Spirit (Jn 3:8)
    B) tongues as of fire (3)
        1) rested on each of the believers
        2) fire often symbolic of God's presence (Ex 3; Hb 10:29)
    C) they were all filled with the Holy Spirit (4)
        1) this is the baptism with the Holy Spirit
        2) distinction between indwelling and filling (control)
        3) empowered to preach gospel worldwide (Ac 1:4-5, 8)
    D) they began to speak with other tongues
        1) as the Holy Spirit gave them utterance/can't be taught
        2) Ryrie—"actual languages unknown to the speakers but
        understood by the hearers" (Ac 2:8)
        3) different from the spiritual gift of tongues which
        requires a spiritual gift to interpret

4) Four Final Comments
    A) test all experiences with God's Word
        —1 Cor 12:1-3; Mt 7:21-23; 1 Jn 4:1-3; 1 Thes 5:21-22
    B) Acts is a transitional period
        —now all believers are baptized with the Holy Spirit at
        conversion (Acts 2:38; 1 Pt 3:21)
    C) Baptism with the Holy Spirit
        1) OT saints were regenerated by the Holy Spirit
        2) OT saints were not normally indwelt by the Holy Spirit
        3) Holy Spirit occassionally came upon some OT saints
        for special empowerment (i.e., annointing of Kings,
        speaking through prophets, etc.)
        4) Spirit baptism is the first filling of the NT believer
        5) one Spirit baptism, many fillings
        6) all NT believers are Spirit baptized
        7) all NT believers are indwelt by Holy Spirit (1 Cor 6:19)
        8) not all believers are filled by the Holy Spirit
    D) the gift of tongues
        1) all believers are now baptized with the Holy Spirit
        2) not all believers have the gift of tongues
            (1 Cor 12:4-13, 28-31)   (1 Cor 1:7; 3:1)
        3) spiritual gifts—not a sign of spiritual maturity
        4) spiritual fruit is a sign of spiritual maturity
            (1 Cor 13:1-4; Gal 5:22-23; Mt 7:21-23)

The Response of the Crowd (Acts 2:5-13)

1) <u>multitudes of Jews staying in Jerusalem</u> (vs 5)
    A) God-seekers from every nation
    B) in Jerusalem for the Feast of Pentecost

2) <u>the crowd was bewildered</u> (vs 6-8)
    A) they heard the sound (like a violent rushing wind)
    B) they each heard the disciples speaking in the languages of the visitors' native lands
    C) they were amazed since the disciples were Galileans
    D) Galileans spoke Aramaic & Greek, but had a strong accent
    E) Matthew 26:73
    F) the disciples were now speaking in many of the different languages of the earth

3) <u>the nations represented by the crowd</u> (vs 9-11)
    A) nations east of the Euphrates River—there Jews spoke
        Aramaic (Jews from the Assyrian deportation of 722BC)
        1) Parthians (from Tigris River to India)
        2) Medes (Media)
        3) Elamites
        4) Mesopotamia
    B) Judea (possibly the wider Judean region-may include Syria)
    C) nations of Asia Minor (modern Turkey)
        1) Cappadocia
        G) Pontus
        H) Asia
        I) Phrygia
        J) Pamphylia
    D) Egypt (northeast tip of Africa)
    E) Libya (northern Africa; west of Egypt)
    F) Cyrene (northern Africa; the capital district of Libya)
    G) Rome (capital of Roman Empire; in Italy; both Jews & proselytes; may have started the church in Rome)
    H) Cretans (Island of Crete in Mediterranean Sea; southeast of Greece)
    I) Arabs (Arabia—to the southeast of Judea)

4) <u>they heard the disciples declare the wonders of God in their own languages</u> (vs 11)

5) <u>they wondered what this meant</u> (vs 12)

6) <u>others mocked the disciples & accused them of being drunk</u> (13)
    A) some will reject God even while witnessing miracles
    B) drunkenness cannot explain this supernatural manifestation

Peter Defends the Actions of the Disciples as the Work of God (Acts 2:14-21)

1) Peter's response—"it's too early in the morning to be drunk"
    (only 9AM; vs 14-15)

2) we must also be willing to defend the work & Word of God

3) <u>this is the work of God</u> (vs 16-21)
    A) this is a partial fulfillment of Joel's prophecy about the Day of the Lord (which will be fulfilled at Christ's return)
    B) the last days began with the first coming of Christ
        (Hebrews 1:1-2; 9:26; 1 Peter 1:20; 1 John 2:18)
    C) the last days end with Jesus' return
    D) the church age is a parenthesis (Daniel's 70 weeks prophecy)
    E) <u>the prophecy of Joel</u> (Joel 2:28-32)
        1) in the last days God will pour out His Spirit on all mankind (not just the Jews—partial fulfillment)
        2) prophecies, visions, dreams will be numerous
        3) signs in the sky (the darkness at the crucifixion was a foreshadowing of the return of Christ—Matthew
        24:29-31; Revelation 6:12-14)
        4) at that point, everyone who calls upon the Lord (Jesus) will be saved
    F) Peter recognized Pentecost as the start of God's last days' outpouring of His Spirit

4) <u>this is the reversal of what God did at the Tower of Babel</u>
    A) <u>Tower of Babel</u>
        1) men united in rebellion against God
        2) God divided their language into numerous languages
    B) <u>Pentecost</u>
        1) men united in their love for God
        2) God opened the doors of communication
    C) learning other languages to unite the world is unbiblical
    D) learning other languages to spread the gospel is dear to the heart of God

5) <u>now, Peter uses this event as an opportunity to preach the gospel</u>
    A) just 50 days earlier Jesus had been crucified
    B) earthquake, darkness, resurrections in Jerusalem, veil torn in the temple
    C) this same crowd was probably in Jerusalem for the
        Passover on which Christ was cruciiifed
    D) they were probably seeking an explanation of those events
    E) now Peter gives God's explanation of the miraculous events that surrounded Christ's death (and life)

Peter Proclaims Jesus' Resurrectio (Acts 2:22-36)

1) <u>Jesus of Nazareth</u> (vs 22-24)
    A) God gave Him His stamp of approval
    B) through miracles (the listeners were aware of this)
    C) He was crucified according to God's foreknowledge & plan
    (Isa 53; Ps 22; Zec 12:10) divine sovereignty/free will
    D) but, God raised Him from the dead
    E) it was not possible for death to hold Him (God, sinless)

2) <u>Peter quotes David—Psalm 16:8-11</u> (vs 25-30)
    A) God would not allow the body of the holy one to see decay
    B) but, David did die; his body decayed
    C) therefore, these words applied to the Messiah—the ultimate
    Son of David & King of Israel
    D) Midrash Tehillim viewed this passage as messianic
    E) a descendent of David would sit on the throne forever
        (Isa 9:6-7; Ps 132:11; 2 Sam 7:12-13; Jer 23:5-6)

3) <u>Peter Proclaims the Resurrection</u> (vs 31-35)
    A) Psalm 16 refered to Jesus, the Jewish Messiah (31)
    B) the apostles & disciples were all witnesses of Jesus'
        resurrection—they saw the resurrected Lord (32)
    C) 1 Corinthians 15:3-8
    D) Jesus is now at the Father's right hand (33-35)
        1) the position of ultimate authority in the universe
        2) Jesus received from the Father the promised Holy
        Spirit
        3) He has poured the Holy Spirit upon His church
        4) this explains the unusual events
        5) David didn't ascend (Psalm 110:1)
        6) David was speaking of the Messiah

4) <u>Peter's Conclusion</u> (vs 36)
    A) all Israel should know with certainty that God has made
    Jesus both Lord & Christ
    B) whom you crucified (non-believing Jews)
    C) Lord = Master (Philippians 2:5-11; name above all other
    names = YHWH)
    D) Christ = the Jewish Messiah; the annointed one; predicted in
    Old Testament; the one who will deliver Israel

5) <u>Conclusion</u>
    A) Jesus proved He is the Jewish Messiah
        —miracles, resurrection, fulfillment of prophecy
    B) Jesus is Lord—is He the Lord over every aspect of your life?

The Result of Peter's Sermon (Acts 2:37-41)

1) The Response of Peter's Hearers (vs 37)
    A) pierced to the heart (convicted for rejecting Christ)
    B) "What shall we do?"—not "What shall we do to be saved?"
    C) good preaching = teaching God's truth with passion
        1) influences the intellect, emotions, & will
        2) encourages, but also convicts hearers
        3) proclaims God's holiness & human sinfulness
        4) it convicts us & calls us to higher spiritual ground
        5) its goal is not to make its hearers feel good
        6) good preaching gives its hearers a sense of God's
        presence—it pierces the heart
        7) Isa 6:1-5; Lk 5:3-10 (the presence of God)

2) Peter Answers His Hearers' Question (vs 38-40)
    A) repent (metanoia = a complete change of heart & action)
    B) there is hope (the gospel is good news)
    C) be baptized (water baptism)
    D) not baptismal regeneration (all converts should be baptized)
    E) in the name of Jesus (in His authority; acknowledges Him)
    F) for the forgiveness of sin (baptism symbolizes inward
    belief)
    G) receive the gift of the Holy Spirit (spirit baptism)
    H) the promise of the Holy Spirit is for you, your children, & all
    who are far off (all mankind-Joel 2:28; Isa 45:22)
    I) all the Lord will call (Jn 6:37-40; 12:32)
    J) Ac 2:21; Joel 2:32 (all who call upon the Lord will be saved)
    K) Peter kept exhorting them with many words
    L) be saved from this perverse generation (their generation had
    rejected Jesus as Messiah & Savior)

3) The Result of Peter's Message (vs 41)
    A) 3,000 were saved (Jn 14:12—greater works)
    B) they received his word (message)
    C) they were water baptized

The First Christian Church (Acts 2:41-47)

1) received the word (41)

2) were baptized

3) they were continually devoted to: (42)
    A) the apostle's teaching (the Old & New Testaments)
    B) fellowship (koinonia; 2 Cor 6:14-18; 1 Jn 1:3)
    C) the breaking of bread (the Lord's Supper—Mt 26:26-28)
    D) to prayer (1 Thes 5:17-118)

4) a sense of awe for God's power (43) 1 Cor 4:21

5) signs & wonders through the apostles (2 Cor 12:11-12)

6) believers had all things in common (44-45)
   A) began selling property & possessions
   B) shared with those in need
   C) not communism (abolition of private property)

7) day by day (46-47)
   A) continued with one mind (unity—Php 2:1-4)
   B) in the temple (probably Solomon's Colonnade)
   C) breaking bread from house to house (cell groups—
         3,000 people can't fit in a house)
   D) ate their meals together (not American overemphasis on
   privacy)
   E) with gladness & sincerity of heart (Php 4:4)
   F) praising God (worship; exalting the God of salvation)
   G) good reputation with outsiders (1 Tim 3:7)
   H) the Lord was adding converts daily

8) Signs of a Healthy Church
   A) convicting preaching (not feel-good messages)
   B) repentance (turning from sin)
   C) evangelistic
   D) baptizes converts
   E) devoted to apostolic teaching (not political correctness;
         not pop psychology)
   F) devoted to fellowship
   G) devoted to the Lord's Supper (focus on Christ's death &
   return)
   H) devoted to prayer
   I) experience God's power (God's life-transforming, lasting
   power)
   J) sharing with one another (not chasing the American dream)
   K) unity—one mind (put others' needs before their own; Jesus'
   agenda comes first)
   L) gathered regularly
         1) large gatherings in the temple
         2) small gatherings in homes
   M) ate meals together
   N) gladness (the joy of the Lord; Neh 8:10)
   O) sincerity of heart/genuine love for one another1 Jn 4:20-21
   P) praising God (worship of God)
   Q) good reputation with outsiders
   R) growing—new converts

Peter & John Heal the Man Born Lame (3:1-26)

1) Introduction
    A) 40 days of post-resurrection appearances of Christ
    B) ascension—wait in Jerusalem for the Holy Spirit
    C) Pentecost—Baptism of the Holy Spirit, 3,000 saved
    D) early church—evangelistic, water baptism, Lord's Supper, apostolic doctrine, fellowship, ministry, prayer, worship

2) Peter & John Heal the Lame Man (vs 1-10)
    A) Peter & John were going to the temple (1)
        1) at the time of prayer
        2) the ninth hour = 3pm
    B) A man who was lame from birth (2-3)
        1) every day he was carried to the temple by friends
        2) he begged temple goers for money
        3) the Beautiful Gate of the Temple
            a) the Nicanor Gate (eastern gate of temple)
            b) led from the Court of the Gentiles to the Women's Court
        4) he asked Peter & John for money
    C) Peter's response (4-6)
        1) Peter had no silver or gold (he was broke)
        2) but he did have Jesus (Aquinas quote—Bruce, 77-78)
        3) he healed the man in the authority of Jesus, not in his own power
        4) in the name of Jesus (name = authority or will)
        5) John 5:43; 6:38; Acts 4:7 (not a magic formula)
        6) "rise & walk"
    D) The lame man is healed (7-10)
        1) Peter & John heal the man (2 Cor 12:12; Hb 2:3-4)
        2) he rises, walks, & begins to leap & praise God in the temple (Isaiah 35:6)
        3) the people in the temple are amazed
    E) Peter used this opportunity to preach the gospel (11-26)
        1) God miraculously heals out of compassion
        2) still, God is more interested in our spiritual well-being than our physical health
        3) each miracle is accompanied by a message (just as it was at Pentecost)
        4) the miracle validates the message of the messenger
    F) Implications of verses 1-10
        1) refutes health & wealth heresy (Rev 2:9; 3:17)
        2) believers, poor or rich, can always share Jesus

            3) God was using signs & wonders to confirm the
                    preaching of the gospel & help the growth of His
        church (1 Cor 4:20)
        4) the only good we can do is in Jesus' authority & power
        (Jn 15:5)

3) Peter Preaches to the People (vs 11-26)
        A) A crowd gathers (11)
            1) around Peter, John, & the healed man
            2) at Solomon's Porch
                a) on the east side of the outer court of the temple
                b) large area with many columns supporting a roof
        B) Not by our power (12)
            1) Zechariah 4:6; 1 Corinthians 10:31
            2) Peter tells the crowd the healing was not by his power
        C) The God of Abraham has glorified Jesus (13-15)
            1) Peter takes the focus off himself & puts it on Jesus
            2) the God of Abraham, Isaac, & Jacob = the God of Israel
            3) God glorified Jesus (resurrection, ascension,
                exaltation)
            4) Jesus = the holy & righteous one; the Prince of Life
            5) the Jews had rejected Jesus & chose Barabbas instead
            6) God raised Jesus from the dead (vindicated Jesus'
            ministry)
            7) we are witnesses (eyewitness testimony)
        D) Jesus healed the lame man (16)
            1) Peter & John did not heal the man through their own
            power
            2) it was the power of the risen Christ that healed the
            man
        E) The Jews rejected Jesus out of ignorance (17)
            1) they did not recognize Jesus as the Jewish Messiah
            2) they were not expecting a suffering Messiah
        F) Old Testament prophets predicted Messiah's sufferings (18)
            1) Peter tells them they should have expected a suffering
Messiah
            2) Isa 52:13-53:12; Ps 22; Zech 12:10; Dan 9:26
        G) A call to repentance (19-21)
            1) repent = turn from their sin of rejecting Jesus
            2) if they trust Jesus for salvation their sins will be
            forgiven
            3) when all Israel accepts Messiah times of refreshing
            will come

               4) Jesus will return to restore all things & rescue Israel

               5) Romans 11:25-27; Zechariah 14:1-5, 9, 11, 16-17

               6) the millennium (Revelation 20:1-6)

     H) <u>Moses called Messiah the ultimate prophet</u> (22-23)

               1) Deuteronomy 18:15, 18-19

               2) one's eternal destiny stands or falls based upon their response to Jesus

     I) <u>Old Testament prophets predicted Messiah's coming</u> (24-25)

               1) from Samuel to his successors (John 5:39-40)

               2) Jesus is the theme of the Old Testament (Lk 24:25-27)

               3) overview of prophecies fulfilled by Jesus

               4) Israel = sons of the prophets & the covenants

               5) Abrahamic Covenant (Genesis 12:1-3)

                    a) Abraham's seed = Jesus (Galatians 3:16)

                    b) all the earth will be blessed (salvation & millennium)

     J) <u>God raised Jesus from the dead</u> (26)

               1) for the Jew first (Jn 4:22; Ac 13:46; Rm 1:16; 2:9-10)

               2) God raised up Jesus/His suffering servant-Ac 2:24, 32

               3) God sent Jesus to turn us from our sinful ways
                    (Lk 19:10)

     K) <u>Conclusion</u>

               1) Peter gave Jesus all the glory (Ephesians 2:8-9;
                    2 Corinthians 10:17)

               2) Christianity is not a new religion; it is the fulfillment or completion of Judaism

               3) Jesus' power is still at work in the world today

               4) when Israel repents Jesus will return

               5) our eternal destiny rests on Jesus' shoulders (Jn 14:6)

Peter & John Arrested (Acts 4:1-22)

1) <u>Introduction</u>

       —Peter & John heal the man born lame & Peter's sermon

2) <u>Peter & John are arrested</u> (vs 1-4)

     A) by the priests

     B) the captain of the temple guard (enforce temple laws)

     C) the Sadducees

               a) they were upset with Peter's message

               b) he proclaimed in Jesus the resurrection

               c) Matthew 22:23-33, 34, 46; Acts 23:6-10

               d) Sadducees—priests, temple, liberal theology (Ac 5:17)

               e) Pharisees—rabbis, synagogues, conservative theology

D) they arrested Peter & John (vs 3)
E) many new converts (vs 4)
    a) due to the healing & Peter's 2nd sermon
    b) now about 5,000 men
    c) up from 3,000 people (Ac 2:41)

3) Peter & John before the Sanhedrin (vs 5-12)
    A) the Sanhedrin = the Jewish ruling council (about 70 rulers, elders, scribes) [5]
    B) Annas the High Priest (6)
        1) the "real" high priest (according to the Jews)
        2) 6AD-15AD (removed by the Romans)
    C) Caiaphas (Mt 26:57; Mk 14:60-62; 15:31)
        1) son-in law of Annas
        2) the "official"high priest (18AD-36AD)
    D) John & Alexander (2 other members of Annas' family)
    E) they questioned Peter & John (7)
        1) by what name or power did you do this? (the healing)
        2) name = authority or power ("in Jesus' name")
    F) Peter's response (vs 8-12)
        1) 2 months earlier he had denied Jesus 3 times
        2) now, filled by the Holy Spirit, things are different
        3) he was respectful ("rulers & leaders")
        4) "we are being tried for healing a man"
        5) Jesus the Messiah
            a) from Nazareth (identifies Jesus)
            b) Jesus healed the man born lame
            c) these rulers crucified Jesus (rejected Him)
            d) but, God raised Him from the dead (accepted Him)
            e) Jesus is the rejected cornerstone
                (Ps 118:22; Isa 28:16; Rm 9:33; Eph 2:19-20;
             1 Pt 2:6-8; Mt 21:42)
        6) salvation in no other name (Jn 14:6; 1 Jn 2:23; Jn 5:23;
    Lk 10:16; Mt 10:32-33; Jn 3:16-18, 36; Php 2:5-11)

4) The Sanhedrin Threatens & Releases Peter & John (vs 13-22)
    A) the council was suprised at confidence of Peter & John (13)
        1) considered them uneducated & untrained men
            a) never attended any recognized rabbinical school
            b) School of Hillel or School of Shammai
        2) they began to recognize them as followers of Jesus
            —Jesus was not an accepted rabbi—but won debates
        3) no attempt to refute the resurrection

B) the council could not refute the fact that a miracle had
taken place—the man had been healed (14)
C) the council ordered Peter & John to temporarily leave their
presence so they could discuss the issue (15)
D) they didn't know what to do with Peter & John (16)
    —they could not deny the reality of the miracle
E) the council decided to warn Peter & John to stop preaching
    Jesus; they wanted to stop the spread of Christianity (17)
F) they ordered Peter & John back into their presence (18)
    1) they ordered them to stop speaking or teaching in the
    name of Jesus
    2) they could talk about God, religion, & morality
    3) they just could not mention the "offensive" name of
    Jesus (Hutcherson, The Church, 89-91, 95)
G) The Response of Peter & John (19-20)
    1) you are supposed to be the religious authorities
    2) you decide if it is right for us to obey men when they
    contradict God
    3) we must obey God rather than men (Acts 5:29)
    4) we cannot stop preaching Jesus
    5) we must proclaim what we have seen & heard
        (1 John 1:1-3; 2 Peter 1:16)
H) the council again threatened Peter & John (21)
    1) then the council released them
    2) no grounds for further punishment
    3) plus, the people were backing Peter & John, &
        glorifying God for the miracle
I) there was no way to explain away the miracle (22)
    —the man born lame was more than 40 years old

5) The Stages of Persecution
    A) ridicule
    B) threats & intimidation
    C) physical persecution (confiscation of property,
        imprisonment, physical harm)
    D) martyrdom (dying for preaching Jesus)
6) Christian Response to Persecution —2 Tm 3:12; Mt 5:11-12; Jm 1:2
7) The Power to Overcome Persecution (Acts 4:31; 5:40-41)

The Apostles Pray For Boldness (Acts 4:23-31)

1) Introduction
- A) Sanhedrin releases Peter & John
- B) ordered them to stop speaking or teaching in Jesus' name

2) Peter & John are released (vs 23)
- A) they return to their fellow believers
- B) they reported what the council had said

3) The believers praise God (vs 24-28)
- A) they lifted their voices to God (24)
- B) with one accord (unity, agreement/Jesus' agenda, not own)
- C) acknowledge God as the sovereign Creator of the universe
- D) Holy Spirit spoke through David (25)
    - 1) dual authorship of Scripture; God guided human authors to record His Word without error
    - 2) they quote from Psalm 2 (viewed as Messianic by Rabbis as early as 100BC)
    - 3) Psalm 2 will be fulfilled after Millennium (Rev 20)
    - 4) the world system is opposed to Christ (Jn 15:18-20; 2 Cor 4:3-4)
    - 5) the nations rage against God & devise futile plans
    - 6) kings & rulers of the earth oppose the Lord & His Christ (26) {refutes Jesus Only movement}
- E) they apply Psalm 2 to their situation (27-28)
    - 1) in Jerusalem (27)
    - 2) Herod, Pilate, Gentiles, & Jews opposed Jesus
    - 3) but they could only do what God predestined (28)
    - 4) their opposition only carried out God's plan (Ac 3:18)
    - 5) God is in control (not the United Nations)

4) The believers ask God for boldness (29-30)
- A) they want God to take note of the council's threats (29)
    —the need for boldness
- B) they ask for ability to speak God's Word with boldness
- C) while God confirms the message with healings, signs, & wonders in Jesus' name (30)

5) God answers their prayer (31)
- A) when they prayed the place was shaken
- B) they were all filled with the Holy Spirit
- C) they began to speak God's Word with boldness

6) Application
- A) importance of prayer (Ac 2:42; 6:4; Cymbala—27-28, 50, 71)
- B) prayer unleashes the power of God (1 Cor 4:20)
- C) guarantee that our prayer will be answered (1 Jn 5:14-15; Mt 7:7-11; Jm 1:5)

D) importance of unity—Jesus is our unity
E) evil world system is opposed to Jesus (Jn 15:18-20)
F) no matter how bad things get, God is in control (His plan cannot be thwarted)
G) be willing to suffer for Jesus (Jn 16:33)
H) when the world tries to intimidate the church into silence, we must ask God for boldness
I) being filled with the Holy Spirit
    1) all believers are indwelt by the Holy Spirit—can't be lost (1 Cor 6:19; Eph 4:30)
    2) not all believers are filled by the Holy Spirit—can be lost, regained, etc. (Ac 2:4; 4:31)
    3) filled by the Holy Spirit = being controlled by the Holy Spirit (Eph 5:18)
J) direct correlation between Spirit-led prayer & being filled with the Holy Spirit

A Community of Unity & Love (Acts 4:32-37)

1) Introduction
    A) the apostles continue to boldly preach Christ's resurrection despite threats from the Jewish ruling council
    B) the apostolic church was devoted to prayer
    C) they were filled with the Holy Spirit
2) True Unity (vs 32)
    A) one heart & soul (complete unity)
        1) they shared the mind/attitude/agenda of Christ
        2) Philippians 2:1-4, 5-11 (put others' needs first)
    B) true unity leads us to share our goods with others
3) The apostles continued to proclaim Jesus' resurrection (vs 33)
    A) with great power & abundant grace (Acts 4:31; Rm 12:6)
    B) power = dunamei / great = megale / grace = charis
4) No needy believers (vs 34-35)
    A) property owners sold their property
    B) donated the money to the apostles
    C) to be distributed to needy believers
    D) due to this, there were no believers in need
    E) the Jerusalem church was a true family of love
    F) eventually, funds ran out & famine set in (Ac 11:28)
    G) the Jerusalem church eventually became dependent on Gentile donations (1 Cor 16:1-3)
    H) true spirituality is no guarantee of material prosperity (Smyrna—Rev 2:9; Laodicea—3:17)

I) <u>not communism</u> (government abolition of private property)
    —religion is opium; attain utopia on earth
J) <u>early church</u>—voluntarily shared private property

5) <u>Barnabas</u> (vs 36-37)
    A) Joseph—called Barnabas (son of encouragement)
    B) a Levite (the priestly tribe; Nm 18:20, 24)
    C) Cyprian by birth (island of Cyprus)
    D) owned land, sold it, gave money to apostles for the needy
    E) would be a great leader of the early church & a colleaugue of the Apostle Paul
    F) some believe Barnabas was the author of Hebrews (Levite)
    G) Barnabas = an example of true spirituality
    H) Ananias & Sapphira (Ac 5)—examples of pseudo spirituality

6) <u>Application</u>
    A) true spirituality helps those in need (Jm 1:27)
    B) true spirituality loves fellow believers (Gal 6:2, 10;
        1 Jn 4:20-21; Mt 25:31-46; Jn 13:34-35)
    C) true spirituality doesn't help the lazy (2 Thes 3:10)
    D) Christian charity, not government welfare (bread &
        circuses)

Our God is a Consuming Fire (Acts 5:1-11)

1) <u>Introduction</u>
    A) a community of unity, love, prayer, God's Word
    B) Barnabas-example of true spirituality
    C) Ananias & Sapphira-examples of pseudo spirituality
    D) though God became a man & died for our sins, He is still God

2) <u>Ananias & Sapphira lie to the Holy Spirit</u> (vs 1-4)
    A) they sold a piece of property
    B) they kept for themselves some of the money
    C) they pretended to give the entire amount to the apostles
    D) Peter told Ananias that he had not lied to men but to God
    E) the Holy Spirit is God (John 14 & 16—the Holy Spirit is a separate Person from the Father & Son)

3) <u>God strikes Ananias dead</u> (vs 5-6)
    A) as Peter spoke, Ananias fell dead
    B) great fear came over all who heard of this
    C) young men quickly buried him

4) <u>God strikes Sapphira dead</u> (vs 7-10)
    A) 3 hours later—Peter questioned Sapphira
    B) she did not yet know of her husband's death
    C) her words proved she was also lying to the Holy Spirit

D) they both had put the Spirit of the Lord to the test
E) Mt 4:5-7; Deut 6:13-17; Ex 17:2
F) arrogance towards God, idolatry, questioning God,
    disobeying God
G) Sapphira immediately fell dead
H) the same young men buried her with her husband

5) <u>Great fear came over the whole church</u> (vs 10)
    A) the fear of the Lord is the beginning of knowledge & wisdom
       (Prov 1:7; 9:10)
    B) perfect love casts out all fear (1 Jn 4:17-18)

6) <u>Conclusion</u>
    A) professing Christians should never put God to the test
    B) refrain from idolatry, arrogance before God,questioning God,
    & disobeying God
    C) we are to be holy as God is holy (1 Peter 1:14-16)
    D) our God is a consuming fire—He is not a pushover
       (Hb 10:28-31; 12:28-29; Rv 3:16)
    E) were Ananais & Sapphira believers?
       1) the Bible does not say
       2) even believers should not test God (1 Cor 11:27-32)
    F) believers must have a personal love relationship with God
    G) still, we should not take God's holiness & justice lightly
    H) He is still the almighty God of Israel
    I)   old expression—if you mess with the bull, you get the horns

Apostolic Signs & Wonders (Acts 5:12-16)

1) <u>Introduction</u>
    A) the apostles & the early church devoted themselves to the
    Word of God, prayer, fellowship, sharing
    B) God judged Ananias & Sapphira

2) <u>Apostolic Signs & Wonders</u> (12-16)
    A) signs & wonders (12)
       1) taking place among the people
       2) these miracles could be verified
    B) <u>in one accord</u> (true unity—Philippians 2:1-4)
    C) <u>Solomon's porch</u>—on temple grounds/large gatherings
       (Acts 5:42—also met in homes)
    D) apostles were respected, but feared (13)
       1) high esteem due to their miraculous works
          & character
       2) fear due to judgment on Ananias & Sapphira

E) <u>apostolic church was growing in number</u> (14)
  1) general rule—churches that manifest the power of God grow in number
  2) not all growing churches are pleasing to God
  3) not all small churches displease God
F) <u>miraculous healings</u> (15-16)
  1) people brought their sick friends to the apostles
  2) the apostles healed the sick through Jesus' power
  3) the apostles also cast demons out of people
    (Mark 6:7-8, 12-13; Acts 1:8)
  4) healing through Peter's shadow?
  5) Holy Spirit worked through the apostles unhindered
  6) 2 Corinthians 12:12; Acts 19:11-12; Mark 5:25-34
3) <u>Conclusion</u>
  A) are we a united church? (true unity is in Christ)
  B) does the world respect us? (1 Timothy 3:7)
  C) does the world fear God because of our church?
    (Proverbs 1:7)
  D) does our church manifest the power of God?
    (1 Corinthians 4:20)
  E) is our church growing? why or why not?
  F) do we hinder the Holy Spirit from working in our lives?
    (1 Thessalonians 5:19-22; Ephesians 4:30)
  G) it is wrong to attempt to copy the apostle's miracles
  H) we should seek the gift-Giver, not the gift
    (1 Corinthians 12:4-11)

Greek Words For Miracles

A) <u>semeion</u>—a sign (Acts 5:12; John 2:18; 20:30-31)
  1) used to denote a miracle as a sign of Divine authority
  2) emphacizes that the miracle points to God
  3) appeals to the intellect (message behind the miracle)
B) <u>teras</u>—a wonder (Acts 5:12)
  1) something strange causing onlookers to marvel
  2) appeals to the imagination
C) <u>dunamis</u>—power (Acts 19:11)
  1) used of works of supernatural origin
  2) emphacizes the power behind the miracle

The Apostles are Arrested (Acts 5:17-42)

1) the high priest & the Saducees were jealous of the popularity of
   the apostles (vs 17; Mk 15:9-10)
2) Caiaphas was the official reigning high priest (18-36AD)
3) however, Annas (6-16AD) really made the decisions
4) the Saducees wanted to be number one
5) they responded to Jesus much like Herod (Mt 2:1-18)
6) the proper response to Jesus
    A) put God first (Mt 6:33; 3 Jn 9-10)
    B) put others before yourself (Php 2:3-4; Mk 10:43-45)
    B) live for Jesus, not for self (2 Cor 5:15; Mk 8:34-35)
    C) do everything for God's glory, not your own (1 Cor 10:31)
7) the Saducees arrested the apostles (vs 18)
    A) earlier, they had arrested Peter & John (Ac 4)
    B) now they arrest all 12 apostles
8) an angel frees the apostles (vs 19-26)
    A) the angel tells the apostles to go to the temple & continue
    preaching about Jesus
    B) the apostles obeyed the angel & preached in the temple
    C) the Sanhedrin heard they were in the temple
    D) the apostles were brought back to the high priest
    E) God does not always miraculously rescue us
        1) Daniel 3:16-18 (Shadrach, Meshach, Abednego)
        2) Mt 26:39 (Jesus)
        3) 2 Cor 12:7-10 (Paul)
    F) we must be content with God's will for our lives
        (1 Jn 5:14-15; Php 4:11-13)
9) the apostles before the Sanhedrin (vs 27-40)
    A) the high priest questioned the apostles (27-28)
    B) he reminded them that they had been ordered to stop
    preaching Jesus
    C) the response of Peter & the apostles (29-32)
        1) we must obey God rather than men
        2) the God of our Fathers (Christianity is Jewish)
        3) God raised Jesus from the dead
        4) the Sanhedrin had Him crucified
        5) God exalted Jesus to His right hand (Ps 110:1)
        6) Jesus is Prince (higher authority than the Sanhedrin)
        7) Jesus is Savior
            a) He can grant repentance to Israel
            b) He can forgive Israel's sins (Jer 31:31, 34)
            c) even the Sanhedrin's sin of killing Jesus
        8) the apostles are witnesses of Christ's resurrection
        9) the Holy Spirit also testifies about Jesus
            (Jn 15:26-27)
        10) to those who really seek God (Jer 29:13)

D) the priests (Saducees) wanted to kill the apostles (vs 33)
E) Gamaliel intervenes (vs 34-39)
 1) Pharisees & Saducees often competed with each other
 2) the Saducees wanted to kill the apostles for
   disobeying their orders
 3) Gamaliel—Hillel's grandson & leader of his school
 4) 2 main ancient rabbinical schools
  a) School of Hillel
  b) School of Shammai (more strict)
 5) Gamaliel—greatest teacher in Israel
 6) Gamaliel—Paul's former teacher (Ac 22:3)
 7) church's complete break with Judaism still future
 8) it was possible to be a Pharisee & be sympathetic to
 the church (Ac 15:5)
 9) Pharisees believed in a future resurrection of
   righteous Jews (Ac 23:6-10)
 10) Gamaliel's advice
  a) not pure pragmatism (Hinduism, Islam, etc.)
  b) given enough time, every false Messiah
    movement will be destroyed by God
  c) Paul disagreed with Gamaliel on this point
  d) Gamaliel—wait & see
  e) Paul—persecute Christians (Php 3:4-6)
  f) 2 failed Messianic movements
   1) Theudas (no other mention of him)
   2) Judas of Galilee (6AD)
    —his followers—the Zealots
  g) the problem with Gamaliel's view
   1) Jesus died, but His movement was
    experiencing more growth than ever before
   2) you can't play the middle of the road—you
  must pick sides (Josh 24:15; 1 Kn 18:21)
F) The Council's Response (vs 40)
 1) they take Gamaliel's advice
 2) they flog the apostles, threaten them, & set them free
G) The Apostles Rejoice (vs 41-42)
 1) they rejoiced they were considered worthy to suffer
 for Jesus (41)
 2) they continued teaching & preaching Jesus (42)
  1) every day (no vacation from serving Jesus)
  2) in the temple (large gatherings)
  3) from house to house (cell groups)
  4) they refused to stop preaching Jesus

H) <u>Conclusion</u>
       1) signs & wonders (2 Cor 12:12)
       2) obey God rather than men (Ac 5:29; Rm 13:1-7)
       3) don't hesitate between 2 positions (Mt 6:24)
       4) consider it an honor to suffer for Jesus
          a) Jm 1:2; 1 Pt 4:12-16; Rm 5:1-5
          b) Jn 15:18-20; 2 Tm 3:12
       5) Christianity—the only Messianic movement still alive
& well after 2,000 years (most didn't last a decade)

The Choosing of the Seven (Acts 6:1-7)

1) <u>Introduction</u>—the apostles would not allow persecution to prevent them from preaching Jesus
2) <u>Increasing in Number</u> (vs 1)
    —because of Acts 5:42 (teaching & preaching Jesus)
3) <u>A Complaint Arose</u> (vs 1)
    A) <u>Hellenistic Jews</u>—primarily Greek-speaking Jews
       1) heavy Greek influence, ties outside Palestine
       2) attended Greek-speaking synagogues
    B) <u>Hebrews</u>—spoke Hebrew (Aramaic) primarily
       1) rejected Greek influence, firmer ties to Palestine
       2) attended Hebrew-speaking synagogues
    C) the Hellenistic Jews believed their widows were being overlooked when the church distributed food for the poor
    D) a serious charge—unlike many complaints in U.S. churches
4) <u>The Solution</u> (vs 2-6)
    A) apostles called an emergency church meeting (2)
    B) <u>first point</u>—apostles refused to neglect their teaching & preaching ministry for the lesser good of feeding the hungry (Lk 10:38-42—Word of God more important than service of others)
    C) <u>second point</u>—seven men must be chosen to distribute the food (3) {Spirit-filled, wise, good reputation}
    D) apostles—devote themselves to Word of God & prayer (4)
    E) the congregation agreed with the apostles (5)
    F) seven Hellenistic Jewish men were chosen (Stephen, Philip, Prochorus, Nicanor, Timon, Parmenas, & Nicolas)
    G) Nicolas was a Gentile convert to Judaism
    H) apostles prayed over & laid hands on the 7 (6) {1 Tm 5:22}
5) <u>The Result</u> (vs 7)
    A) the Word of God kept spreading
    B) number of disciples in Jerusalen increased greatly
    C) many of the priests accepted Christ (not the chief-priests who led the Sanhedrin)

6) Important Principles from this Passage
        A) preaching Jesus brings results (Isa 55:11; Rm 1:14-17)
        B) every church faces challenges & struggles
        C) a church needs God's wisdom to work through its problems
        D) Pastor must focus on God's Word & prayer in his ministry
        E) Pastor must equip people for service (Eph 4:11-15)
        F) church leadership must be Spirit-filled
        G) church decisions must be made prayerfully
        H) churches grow when there is true unity
        I) churches must try to meet the physical needs of their people
        (not just spiritual needs; Jm 1:27)

Preaching the Gospel
1) the problem is not the Gospel
2) the problem is our lack of faith in the power of the Gospel to save
       & transform lives

Future Offices in the Early Church
1) elders/overseers (1 Timothy 3:1-7; lead & teach)
2) deacons (1 Timothy 3:8-13; serve; diakonia—Acts 6:1, 2)
3) widows (1 Timothy 5:3-16; no living relatives; devotes life to
       prayer; church supports her)

The Pastor's Role:
1) he is not primarily a full-time counselor, philanthropist, c.e.o.,
       administrator, or teacher
2) he is primarily a full-time equipper of the saints for service (this is
       accomplished through prayer, studying God's Word,
       preaching, & teaching)
3) the pastor is not to do all the ministry himself, but to equip the
       saints to do the work of ministry
4) Pastor Tangeman's book (page 227)

Stephen is Arrested (Acts 6:8-15)

1) Introduction
        A) 7 deacons are chosen to oversee the food distribution for
        the Hellenistic Jewish widows
        B) Stephen was one of the 7 chosen
        C) many temple priests accepted Christ (Ryrie—Mt 27:51?)
2) God worked miracles through Stephen (vs 8)
        A) full of grace (charitos = grace for gifts; Rm 12:6)
        B) full of power (dunamos; 1 Cor 4:20)
        C) wonders (terata = something strange or unusual causing
        onlookers to marvel)
        D) signs (semeia = emphacizes the Divine message behind the
        miracle; the miracle points to God)
        E) great = megala (mega—describes both signs & wonders)

F) among the people (not behind closed doors like today's
        pseudo miracles)
G) God was confirming the early preaching of the Gospel with
signs & wonders (2 Cor 12:12; Hb 2:3-4; Ac 7:36)

3) <u>Stephen receives opposition</u> (vs 9-12)
    A) <u>the opposition</u> = the Synagogue of the Freedmen (9)
        1) former Jewish slaves or sons of slaves who were set
    free; they were originally from:
                a) Cyrene (northern Africa)
                b) Alexandria (Egypt, northern Africa)
                c) Cilicia (NE of Israel, near Mediterranean Sea)
                d) Asia (area of modern Turkey)
        2) they argued with Stephen in the synagogue (they were
    probably Hellenistic Jews)
        3) synagogue = a local assembly of Jews where Old
            Testament was taught
        4) at this time the church had not completely broken off
    from Judaism (still met in synagogues)
    B) they could not refute Stephen's teachings (vs 10)
        —due to the divine wisdom which the Holy Spirit gave to
    Stephen (Lk 21:12-15)
    C) they secretly persuaded others to falsely testify against
    Stephen—blasphemus words against Moses & God (11)
    D) they stirred up the people, the elders, & the scribes (12)
        1) they dragged Stephen to the council
        2) council = the Sanhedrin (70 elders who ruled over
        Jewish religious matters)

4) <u>Stephen on trial before the Sanhedrin</u> (vs 13-15)
    A) false witnesses claimed he constantly spoke out against the
temple & the Mosaic Law (13)
        —Jesus' coming signaled the end of the temple order
    B) <u>Jesus the Nazarene</u> (from Nazareth) (14)
        1) they claimed Jesus said He would destroy the temple
    (Jn 2:19-21; Mk 14:58; Mt 24:1-2; Mt 12:6)
        2) they claimed Jesus would change the ceremonial
    aspects of the Law of Moses (Jn 4:19-24;
        Rm 3:19-24; 6:14; 10:4)
        3) temple—not only a religious issue in Jerusalem, but
    also an economic issue
        4) Stephen understood (better than most early believers)
    that Christ's coming would drastically change the
    religious life of the Jews
        5) things would never again be the same
            (new wine—Mt 9:17)
    C) Stephen's face was like the face of an angel (15)
        —God miraculously vindicated Stephen in the midst of
    his persecution (Moses—Ex 34:29-30, 33-35)

5) <u>Conclusion</u>
      A) Jesus fulfilled the temple ministry & the Old Testament ceremonial law
      B) Gal 3:24-25; Col 2:16-17; Hb 10:1, 11-14
      C) Old Testament Law/Law of Moses
            1) ceremonial aspects (fulfilled by Christ)
            2) civil aspects (applied only to Israel as a nation)
            3) moral aspects (still applies to all mankind today)
      D) purpose of the Law—not to save, but to show us our need for a Savior (Romans 3:20)
      E) we should not get so caught up in religious tradition that we lose sight of the substance—Jesus Himself
      F) when we boldly preach Jesus, persecution will come
      G) the Gospel is more than words, it is God's power to save & transform lives (Rm 1:16)
      H) sometimes God chooses to display this power through miraculous signs

Stephen's Final Sermon (Acts 7:1-53)

1) <u>Introduction</u> (vs 1)
      A) charges against Stephen—speaking against Temple & Law
      B) high priest—probably Caiaphas
          —reigned until 36AD; presided over Jesus' trial
      C) Caiaphas asked Stephen if the charges were true
      D) the temple, not the Messiah had become the focal point of the Jewish religion
2) <u>Stephen's Sermon</u> (vs 2-53)
      A) not in defense of himself—not trying to get acquitted
      B) rather, it was in defense of the Christian Faith
      C) <u>major themes of his sermon</u>
            1) God's presence not restricted to any one location (48)
                a) God called Abraham long before he moved to the Holy Land
                b) God was with Joseph in Egypt
                c) God gave Israel the Mosaic Law in the wilderness
            2) the Jew's continued rejection of God's messengers
                a) Joseph's brothers rejected him
                b) many Jews opposed Moses in the wilderness
                c) the Jews persecuted their own prophets
                d) the Jews rejected & killed their Messiah
                e) now, they were rejecting Stephen for proclaiming Jesus
                f) now they were doing just what their descendants had done—opposing the work of God

D) Outline of Stephen's Sermon
    1) the Patriarchs (vs 2-8)
        —Abraham, Isaac, Jacob, 12 sons (the fathers of the Jewish nation)
    2) Joseph (vs 9-19) Israel in Egypt
    3) Moses (vs 20-43) wilderness wandering
    4) Tabernacle & Temple (vs 44-50)
        a) God's presence is not restricted to one location
        b) vs 48; John 4:19-26
    5) Israel murdered her prophets & her Messiah (vs 51-53)
E) Stephen discusses Israel's history before the temple
F) Israel had a spiritual history before the temple
G) Israel will have a spiritual history after the temple
H) the temple is not essential to true worship
3) The Patriarchs (vs 2-8)   [the fathers of the Jewish nation]
    A) hear me brethren & fathers (2)
        1) Stephen was respectful to his opponents
            (Eph 4:15; 1 Pt 3:15)
        2) Stephen was Jewish—one of their countrymen
        3) although he was a Hellenistic Jew
    B) the God of glory
        1) appeared to Abraham (father of the Jewish nation)
        2) while Abraham was in Mesopotamia (not Israel)
        3) God's glory was not restricted to the holy land, the tabernacle, or the temple (shekinah glory cloud)
    C) God commanded Abraham to leave his country & family (3)
        —to go into the promised land (Canaan; future Isreal)
    D) Abraham obeyed (4)
        1) he left the land of the Chaldeans (ancient Babylon)
        2) after settling in Haran, he moved to the holy land
        3) Abraham's father—Terah
    E) Abraham owned no piece of the promised land (5)
        1) he was an alien in the land of Canaan
        2) he was elderly & had no child
        3) but God promised him that he would have a son & that the promised land would be given to his
            descendants
    F) God predicted Israel's 400 years of bondage in Egypt (6-7)
        1) they would be enslaved in Egypt for 400 years
        2) God would judge Egypt (10 plagues, Red Sea)
        3) God would free the Israelites
        4) the Israelites would serve God in the promised land

G) God gave Abraham the covenant of circumcision (8)
    1) covenant = agreement, pact, treaty
    2) circumcision = removal of the foreskin
        a) it separated Jews from Gentiles
        b) it symbolized the entrance into the community
        of faith (Rm 4:9-12; 2:28-29)
    3) the fathers of the Jewish nation
        a) Abraham
        b) Isaac (the promised son)
        c) the 12 patriarchs (heads of 12 tribes of Israel)
H) the main points of verses 2-8
    1) God's glory was not limited to the temple or promised land
    2) Abraham was not a citizen of the Holy Land
    3) the Jews lived in Egyptian bondage for 400 years
    4) circumcision came before the temple & Mosaic Law
    5) Israel—God's community of faith (not the temple/law)

4) <u>Stephen Speaks About Joseph</u> (vs 9-19)
    A) <u>Introduction</u>—2 main points of Stephen's defense
        1) God's presence not restricted to one location
        2) the Jews' continued rejection of God's messengers
    B) <u>Joseph</u> (9-19)
        1) patriarchs = Joseph's 10 brothers/Benjamen not
            included (9)
        2) became jealous of Joseph & sold him into slavery
        3) the Jews had a history of opposing God's messengers
        4) Joseph ended up in Egypt
        5) still, God was with him (no temple/outside Jerusalem)
        6) God rescued him from all his sufferings (10)
            —slavery & imprisonment
        7) Pharoah made Joseph govenor over all Egupt
        8) famine in Egypt & Canaan (11)
            a) the Jewish patriarchs could find no food
            b) Jacob sent his sons to Egypt for food (12)
            c) on their 2nd visit to Egypt (13-14)
                1) Joseph revealed his identity to his
                    brothers (the Jewish nation will not
                    recognize Jesus until their 2nd meeting)
                2) Pharoah accepted Joseph's family
                3) 75 persons in all (Jacob, 12 sons, & their
            families)
        9) the Jewish patriarchs died in Egypt (15)
            —not in the promised land
        10) eventually, their remains were buried in Canaan (16)
            —in the tomb Abraham bought in Shechem
        11) still, the Jews multiplied in Egypt (17)
            —God blessed them outside the promised land

12) finally a Pharoah came to power who did not
   remember Joseph & the debt Egypt owed to him (18)
   a) he enslaved the Jews (19)
   b) he ordered that newborn Jewish males be
   drowned in the Nile River
13) this gave the Jews incentive to leave Egypt
   —sometimes God has to make us uncomfortable
   where we are so that we have the incentive
   to go where we need to be (in His will)

Overview of Joseph's Life (Genesis 37-50)
1) Joseph in Canaan
   A) the oldest son of Jacob's favorite wife-Rachel
   B) Joseph was Jacob's favorite son
   C) he gave Joseph a multi-colored cloak (royalty)
   D) his hard-working brothers were jealous
      1) once he told his father they weren't working
      hard
      2) he dreamed they would bow before him
      3) they sold him into slavery to traders
      4) they told Jacob he was killed by wild beasts
      5) Joseph ended up a slave in Egypt
2) Joseph earned the trust of Potiphar
   A) Potiphar-an officer of Pharoah
   B) he made Joseph an overseer of his house
   C) Potiphar's wife tempted Joseph to have sex with her
   D) Joseph refused/fled naked when she grabbed his cloak
   E) Potiphar's wife accused Joseph of rape
   F) Joseph was arrested & sent to prison
3) Joseph in prison
   A) he interpreted the dreams of Pharoah's cupbearer &
   baker (they had been imprisoned)
   B) the cupbearer would be released & get his job back
   C) the baker would be executed
   D) the cupbearer forgot Joseph & Joseph remained in
   prison (13 years of slavery & imprisonment)
4) Pharoah's dream
   A) no one could interpret it
   B) the cupbearer remembered Joseph
   C) Joseph interpreted the dream
   D) the dream—7 years of plenty & 7 years of famine
5) Joseph was released from prison
   —Pharoah put him in charge of food collection & food
   distribution (Joseph was 2nd in command in Egypt)

6) Joseph & his family are reunited

    A) Jacob sent his sons to Egypt for food during the famine

    B) Joseph revealed his identity to his brothers on their 2nd visit

    C) Joseph's brothers & family settle in Egypt

    D) they are treated well by Egypt until a Pharoah came to power who did not know of the debt Egypt owed to Joseph & his descendants

5) Stephen Speaks About Moses (vs 20-43)

    A) Moses' first 40 years (vs 20-29)

        1) Moses' birth & first 3 months (20)

            a) Moses' parents refused to put him in the Nile

            b) they cared for him at home for 3 months

        2) Pharoah's daughter adopted Moses (21)

        3) Moses' education & reputation (22)

        4) Moses attempts to deliver Israel (23-24)

        5) Israel rejects Moses the first time (25-28)

            —Moses is a type of Christ

        6) Moses fled to Midian (29)

            a) he was an alien in that land

            b) as the patriarchs were in Canaan

            c) Moses' 2 sons were born there (not in Holy Land)

    B) Moses' second 40 years (vs 30-34)

        1) God appears to Moses in a burning bush (30)

            a) at Mount Sinai (not in Holy Land)

            b) Moses was about 80 years old

            c) angel = messenger (this messenger is God)

            d) burning bush = the presence of God

        2) angel speaks with the voice of the Lord (31)

        3) angel identifies Himself as the God of Abraham, Isaac, & Jacob (32)

        4) holy ground—outside Jerusalem & Holy Land (33)

        5) God saw Israel's suffering in Egypt (34)

            a) God relates to His people outside Holy Land

            b) God would use Moses as His instrument to deliver Israel

            c) in a far away land, God hears the cries of His people

C) <u>Moses' last 40 years</u> (vs 35-43)
    1) Moses had been rejected the first time by his people
    2) God sent His appointed deliver a second time (35)
        —Moses is a type of Christ
    3) Moses' deliverance was accepted by Israel the second
    time (36)
        a) he led Israel our of Egypt
        b) he performed wonders & signs
        c) in Egypt, Red Sea, & wilderness (not Holy Land)
        d) 40 years of wilderness wandering
            1) Jews refused to enter Promised land
            2) Israel postponed her blessing 80 years
    4) Moses predicted the Messiah would come (37)
        a) he refered to Him as the prophet
        b) He would be a Jew
    5) God spoke to Moses & Israel in the wilderness (38)
        —God can speak to His people outside Holy Land
    6) Israel constantly rejected Moses (39)
        a) Moses was a type of Christ
        b) their hearts turned back to Egypt (the world)
    7) Israel worshiped the golden calf (40-41)
        a) they had a history of rejecting the true God & His
    messengers
        b) they rejoiced in their man-made religious
            project (what the temple had become)
    8) God delivered Israel over to idolatry (42-43)
        a) astrology = worship of stars & planets
        b) Moloch = Canaanite false god; human sacrifices
        offered to him
        c) Rompha = false god; the planet Saturn
        d) Babylonian captivity predicted
        e) Romans 1:24, 26, 28
        f) Israel often rejected the true God & His
            appointed messengers
        g) it is no suprise they rejected their Messiah &
        now Stephen
6) <u>Stephen Finishes His Sermon</u> (vs 44-50)
    A) <u>the tabernacle/temple</u> (vs 44-47)
        1) <u>major themes of his sermon</u> (Acts 7)
            a) God's presence-not restricted to any one location
            b) Jews' continued rejection of God's messengers

2) <u>wilderness</u> (44) {1450-1410BC}
        a) the Jews had the tabernacle in the wilderness
        b) tabernacle = portable temple
        c) tent of testimony (contained the stone tablets)
        d) Hebrews 9:1-5; 23-24
        e) built by God's directions (Ex 25:9, 40; Hb 8:2)
        f) later, temple was built by man's initiative
        g) notes on temple & furniture (fulfilled in Christ)
3) <u>Joshua</u> (45)
        a) tabernacle brought into Promised Land when
        Joshua conquered the Canaanites (1410BC)
        b) still no stationary temple
4) <u>David</u> (45-46) {2nd King of Israel—around 1,000BC}
        a) still no temple (though David wanted to build it)
        b) God was pleased with David's request
        c) but told him his son would build the temple
        d) David's reign was a bloody reign
        e) Mk 11:17; Jn 3:17; 1 Chron 17:1-15
5) <u>Solomon</u> (47) {3rd King of Israel}
        a) 966BC—temple is finally built
        b) he knew temple could not contain God-1 Kn 8:27
        c) 1 Chron 22:6-10; 2 Chron 6:14, 15, 18, 41-42
        d) ultimate fulfillment-Christ (Lk 1:32-33; Ezk 40)
B) <u>God's Presence</u> (48-50) {God is the omnipresent Creator}
    1) no one location can contain Him
    2) Isa 66:1-2; Ac 17:24; Jn 4:20-24
C) <u>Stephen's View of the Temple</u>
    1) opposed to worshiping the temple
    2) even worship in the temple is not sufficient
    3) don't make an idol out of the temple
    4) don't limit God's presence to the temple
    5) don't miss what the temple points to—Jesus
    6) history of God's special presence (the manifestation
of His glory)
        a) in nature (Psalm 19:1) perverted by the nations
        b) Christophanies to the Patriarchs (Gn 12-37)
        c) the tabernacle (Ex)
        d) the temple (1 Kn & 2 Chron)
        e) Jesus (Jn 2)
        f) all believers (1 Cor 6:19)
    7) God is omnipresent—He can manifest Himself in a
special way, but is not restricted to the temple
    8) the temple is not essential to God's presence or for
God's work or worship of God

7) <u>Stephen Accuses His Persecutors</u> (vs 51-53)
    A) stiff-necked; Ex 32:1-5, 9 (vs 51)
        1) like an ox or horse that won't respond to the reigns
        2) Israel had a history of resisting God
    B) uncircumcised in heart & ears (Jer 9:26; Rm 2:28-29)
    C) always resisting the Holy Spirit
        —Hb 3:7-11; Mt 23:37-38 (free will)
    D) doing what their fathers did (Mt 23:29-35)
        1) they persecuted the prophets (vs 52)
        2) they killed those who announced Christ's coming
            —Isaiah, Jeremiah, Zechariah, John the Baptist
        3) they betrayed & murdered Christ
            a) the Righteous One = dikaios
            b) Ac 3:13-14; Isa 53:11; Jer 23:5-6; 1 Pt 3:18
    E) they did not keep the Law (vs 53)
        1) they received the Law (EX 20)
        2) ordained by angels (Gal 3:19; Hb 2:2; Hb 1:1-4)
        3) they did not keep the Law (Rm 3:20; Hb 10:28-29)
    F) <u>application</u>
        1) are we, like Stephen, willing to suffer for Jesus?
            a) Jn 15:18-20; 2 Tm 3:12
            b) 160,000 Christians currently martyred each year
            c) Temple University (Corpus Christi play)
        2) is the American church in the same state as Stephen's
persecutors?
            a) do we stubbornly resist God's will?
            b) are we spiritually circumcised/baptized?
            c) do we reject God's messengers?
            d) do we obey God's laws (Jm 2:26)
        3) Jesus cleansed His temple; He will also clean
        His church (1 Peter 4:17)
8) <u>The Death of Stephen</u> (vs 54-60)
    A) Stephen acted as if he was prosecutor, not defendant (54)
    B) he accused his accusers of idolatry (temple) & murder
        (Jesus & the prophets)
    C) the Jewish religious leaders were filled with rage & anger
    D) gnashing their teeth (extreme distaste - Mt 13:41-42)
    E) <u>Stephen was full of the Holy Spirit</u> (55-56)
        1) he was controlled by the Holy Spirit (not just indwelt)
        2) gazed into heaven (a vision)
        3) he saw the glory of God (shekinah - real temple)
        4) Jesus standing at the Father's right hand
            —Jesus rules the universe
        5) Mk 14:61-64 (Jesus' trial)

6) the Son of Man (Jesus—80 times; once in rest of NT)
      a) evidence for antiquity of this event
      b) Jesus' favorite title (heavenly King-Dan 7:13-14)
7) Stephen told onlookers what he saw
8) Jesus standing, not sitting (standing ovation, greet?)

F) The Stoning of Stephen (57-60)
    1) they rushed Stephen (57)
      a) cried out & covered their ears (demonic rage)
      b) they considered what he said blasphemous
    2) they drove him out of the city (58)
      a) didn't want to defile the city
      b) they began stoning him
      c) witnesses left their robes with a young man named Saul (Paul)
      d) Paul-Sanhedrin member? (Ac 26:10)
      e) witnesses = martures
      f) ironically, Stephen was first Christian martyr
    3) Stephen's last words (59-60)
      a) spoken as he was being stoned
      b) almost direct quotes from Jesus (Lk 23:46, 34)
      c) "Lord Jesus, receive my spirit"
         1) calls Jesus Lord (Kurios = Yahweh)
         2) treats Jesus as equal to God (Ps 31:5)
      d) he asks that God forgives his murderers
         —at least one of Stephen's murderers was eventually forgiven (Saul/Paul)
      d) he fell asleep = he died
    4) Conclusion (Ac 8:1-4) love Jesus more than life
      a) great persecution began against the church
      b) believers scattered, but preached gospel
      c) Jn 15:18-20; 16:2; 2 Tm 3:12; Lk 21:12-17
      d) Mt 10:32-33; 2 Cor 5:15 (live for Jesus, not self)

The Persecuted Church Begins to Spread the Gospel
(Acts 8:1-4)

1) Introduction
   A) Stephen had just been stoned to death for preaching Christ
   B) Saul was in total agreement with the execution

2) Saul the Persecutor (vs 1-3)
   A) Saul agreed with the stoning of Stephen
      1) Stephen's killers laid their cloaks at Saul's feet
         -he have overseen the execution (7:58)
      2) Saul was from Tarsus in Cilicia (9:11)
         a) he may have debated Stephen in the synagogue
            (6:8-13)
         b) Saul was a Pharisee (Php 3:5)
         c) now some Pharisees were joining the
            Sadducees in persecuting the church
            (Ac 9:1-2)
   B) Saul was leading house to house searches for Christians &
      imprisoning them (1 Tm 1:12-15)
      1) made havoc = elumaineto = to devestate; a ravaging
         of a body by a wild beast
      2) a great persecution arose against the church in
         Jerusalem (both men & women persecuted)
      3) primarily against Hellenistic Jewish Christians?
         a) after this point the Jerusalem Church was
            predominately Hebrew
         b) Hellenistic believers were thought to be anti-
            temple & opposed to the Mosaic Law
      4)Christians fled & were scattered (diesparesan;
         diaspora) throughout Judea & Samaria
      5) except for the apostles
         a) popularity of the apostles?
         b) not Hellenistic Jews?

        c) they remained in Jerusalem to continue
          preaching God's Word
        d) they may have been in hiding (the church was
          forced underground) Ac 9:26-27
   C) devout men buried Stephen & mourned for him

3) <u>The Scattered Believers Spread the Gospel</u> (vs 4)
      A) scattered = diasparentes (diaspora)
      B) persecution does not destroy God's church (Ac 11:19-21)
      C) the church grows in the midst of persecution
      D) Tertullian-3rd century AD-"the blood of the martyrs is the
      seed of the church."

4) <u>Conclusion</u>
      A) persecution forced believers out of Jerusalem & into
         Judea & Samaria (Ac 1:8)
      B) God often brings good results out of bad circumstances
      C) Rm 8:28; Gn 50:20
      D) the persecution aided jumpstarted the spread of the Gospel
      E) often we must be taken out of our comfort zones before
         we are ready to serve God (me-NJ/USMC/WA)
      F) when the church is sought out & devoured, it seeks out &
         devours for God's Kingdom
      G) <u>God is the God of a second chance </u>(Ac 20:19-21)
         -Saul the persecutor eventually became Paul the
apostle,   missionary, evangelist, theologian, apologist, NT
         author, saint, & martyr
      H) God is in the business of bringing good out of evil

The Gospel is Preached in Samaria (Acts 8:4-17)

1) Introduction (vs 4)
  A) after Stephen's execution, Saul began to persecute the
      church
  B) believers were scattered & began to preach the Gospel
2) Philip Preaches the Gospel in Samaria (vs 5-8)
  A) Philip = one of the 7 deacons of Acts 6:5 (vs 5)
  B) the city of Samaria (probably the ancient capital of the
      Israel which had been conquered by the Assyrians)
  C) the strife between the Jews & Samaritans (722BC)
  D) Jesus had already preached in the region of Samaria (Jn 4)
  E) Jesus tears down walls that divide people (Eph 2:11-14)
  F) Philip preached Christ to the Samaritans
      1) Christ is the Gospel; Christ is Christianity
      2) not true for Buddhism, Hinduism, Islam, Judaism . . .
  G) the entire multitude professed faith in Christ (vs 6-7)
      1) because they saw the miracles Philip performed
      2) he cast out demons
      3) he healed the lame & the paralyzed
  H) there was great joy in the city (vs 8)
      -the joy of being saved (so absent in today's church)
3) Simon the Sorcerer (vs 9-13)
  A) Simon who practiced sorcery (9-11)
      1) early church fathers called him Simon Magus
      2) they said he was one of the founders of Gnosticism
          a) he believed in a series of divine emanations
              called powers
          b) Simon claimed to be one of the higher powers
          c) he amazed people with his occult powers
  B) sorcery = mageuon (verb for doing magic)
      1) secret, occultic, magical powers
      2) magi of Mt 2 were probably Zoroastrian astrologers

3) magi blended science with the occult

4) not pharmakia (utilizes incantations & drugs)

C) the Samaritans believed Philip's message & were water baptized (vs 12) {superior miracles; power encounter}

D) Simon also "believed" (vs 13)

1) mere mental assent?

2) wrong motives? (desire for spiritual power)

3) true saving faith (Jm 2:14-26; Mt 7:21-23)

4) <u>Peter & John Investigate the Situation</u> (vs 14-17)

A) the apostles send Peter & John to investigate (14)

1) the unity of the church (Jew/Samaritan/Gentile)

2) only one church--the apostolic church

B) Peter & John baptized the new converts with the Holy Spirit (15)

C) they had only been water baptized in the name of Jesus; they had yet to receive the Holy Spirit (16)

D) Peter & John laid hands on them for them to receive the Holy Spirit (17)

E) this event doesn't justify the modern Pentecostal emphasis

F) God delayed Holy Spirit baptism:

1) to confirm the reality of the Samaritan conversions for the apostles (same experience as the Jews)

2) to confirm the unity of the church

G) now we are baptized with the Holy Spirit at the moment we first believe (Eph 1:13-14; 1 Cor 12:13; Mt 3:11-12)

5) <u>Conclusion</u>

A) Jesus came to save all people (Isa 45:22)

B) we are to preach Jesus in all the world (Mt 28:19-20)

C) God is more powerful than Satan (1 Jn 4:4)

D) we cannot fellowship with demons (2 Cor 6:14-18)

Peter Confronts Simon the Sorcerer (Acts 8:18-25)

1) Introduction
   A) Philip, after fleeing persecution, preached the gospel in
      Samaria (Philip performed miracles there)
   B) many Samaritans accepted the gospel & were baptized
   C) even Simon the Sorcerer was baptized
   D) Peter & John came to investigate the situation
   E) they baptized the converts with the Holy Spirit

2) Manifestations that Accompanied Baptism with the Holy Spirit
   A) when new groups of people were added to the church
   B) start of the church at Pentecost (Acts 2)
   C) Samaritans (Acts 8)
   D) Gentiles (Cornelius; Acts 10, 11)
   E) followers of John the Baptist (Acts 19)
   F) God emphasized the unity of the church

3) Simon the Sorcerer Tries to Buy Spiritual Power From the
   Apostles (vs 18-19)
   A) Peter & John laid hands on the new believers & baptized
      them with the Holy Spirit
   B) Simon the Sorcerer saw the external signs that
      accompanied Holy Spirit baptism
   C) he only believed because he wanted spiritual power
   D) he offered to pay the apostles for the power to baptize
      others with the Holy Spirit

4) Peter Confronts Simon the Sorcerer (vs 20-23)
   A) your money perish with you (20)
      1) Simon wasn't really saved
      2) Simon thought the gift of God could be bought with
         money

3) Simony = the buying or selling of religious
    privileges
B) your heart is not right with God (21)
    1) Simon was not really saved
    2) he had no portion in God's work or kingdom
C) repent of your wickedness & pray for forgiveness (22)
D) Simon's spiritual condition (23)
    1) poisoned by bitterness
    2) bound by iniquity (Romans 6:17-18)

5) <u>Simon the Sorcerer's Response</u> (vs 24)
    A) pray for me
    B) fear of God's judgment
    C) no thought of battling Peter

6) <u>What Became of Simon the Sorcerer?</u>
    A) the founder of the false "gnosis" (1 Timothy 6:20)
        1) the earliest stage of Gnosticism?
        2) salvation through the knowledge of hidden secrets
    B) Simon called himself the power of God
    C) he redeemed a slave girl named Helena & claimed she was
        the first idea generated by him
    D) Simon developed a mystical, complex system of theology
        with numerous intermediaries between God & man
    E) he had a mystical method of interpreting Scripture
    F) he had his followers bury him alive & promised to rise on
        the third day (he failed to keep his promise)
    G) his followers were called the Simonians & survived until
        the third century
    H) Justin Martyr, Irenaeus, Tertullian, Hippolytus

7) <u>Peter & John Complete Their Mission</u> (vs 25)
    A) they preached God's Word in that city & throughout many
       villages of Samaria
    B) they returned to Jerusalem

8) <u>Conclusion</u>
    A) we must believe in Jesus for the right reason
       -for salvation, not power or money
    B) heresy must be refuted & truth must be defended
    C) wolves in sheep's clothing must be exposed (Jude 3, 4)
    D) true saving faith will produce good works (James 2:26;
       Matthew 7:15, 21-23)

Philip Leads the Ethiopian Eunuch to Christ (Acts 8:26-40)

1) Introduction
   - A) persecution caused many believers to flee Jerusalem
   - B) Philip fled to Samaria & preached Jesus there
   - C) Peter & John baptized the Samaritan converts with the
          Holy Spirit; Peter confronted Simon the Sorcerer
   - D) now Philip preaches Jesus to an Ethiopian Eunuch
2) An angel directs Philip to go south (vs 26)
   - A) to the road from Jerusalem to Gaza
   - B) Gaza-southwest of Jerusalem, by the Mediterranean Sea
   - C) the last settlement before the desert area that led to Egypt
   - D) the road most travelers took to Africa
3) Philip meets the Ethiopian Eunuch (vs 27-29)
   - A) Philip immediately obeyed the angel
   - B) eunuch (emasculated or just a government official?)
   - C) Ethiopia (a nation of Africa)
   - D) great authority-in charge of the Queen's treasury
   - E) Queen Candace
        1) in Ethiopia, the king was considered the son of the
              sun & too holy to bother with political matters
        2) his mother ruled in his place
   - F) the Ethiopian was returning from worshiping in Jerusalem
   - G) a proselyte or a God-fearer?
   - H) he was reading from Isaiah 53
   - I) the Holy Spirit told Philip to approach his chariot
4) Philip explains Isaiah 53 to the Eunuch (vs 30-35)
   - A) the Ethiopian asks Philip to interpret Isaiah 53 for him
   - B) the Ethiopian wondered of whom the passage spoke
   - C) Philip began with Isaiah 53 & preached Jesus to him
   - D) Isaiah 52:13-53:12 (the suffering servant; written 700BC)
   - E) Edith Schaeffer-*Christianity is Jewish* (pages 13-14)

5) <u>The Ethiopian believes in Jesus & is baptized</u> (vs 36-39)
    A) he was baptized immediately after believing (see Acts 2)
    B) baptism by immersion?
6) <u>The Holy Spirit snatches Philip away</u> (vs 39)
    A) caught = harpazo (same word for rapture in 1 Thess 4)
    B) the Eunuch saw him no more
    C) the Eunuch returned to Ethiopia rejoicing
    D) Irenaeus (130-202AD) wrote that the Eunuch became a
        missionary to his own people
7) <u>Philip continued preaching Jesus</u> (vs 40)
    A) the Holy Spirit took Philip to Azotus for another mission
    B) Azotus-20 miles north of Gaza
    C) Philip preached there & continued to preach in all the
        cities he passed through as he headed north, finally
        settling in Caesarea (60 miles north of Azotus)
    D) Philip settled in Caesarea (Acts 21:8-9; 20 years later)
8) <u>Conclusion</u> (principles we can apply from this historical event)
    A) only apply principles clearly taught elsewhere in Scripture
    B) Jesus fulfilled Old Testament Messianic prophecies
    C) teachers of the Word are needed
    D) we, like Philip, must be led by the Holy Spirit
    E) we, like Philip, must be prepared to share our faith
    F) we, like Philip, have a role in the Great Commission
        (Mt 28:19-20; go, make disciples, baptize, teach)
    G) true salvation brings joy (Php 4:4; 1 Thes 5:16; Neh 8:10)
    H) God can use us even when we're on the run
        1) He can use us when our whole world is coming apart
        2) He can use us when our enemies are hunting us
           down
        3) when we are weak, He is strong (2 Cor 12:9)

The Conversion of Saul (Acts 9:1-9)

1) Introduction
    A) persecution against Hellenistic Jewish Christians forced them to flee Jerusalem
    B) Saul approved of Stephen's stoning (one of the 7 deacons)
    C) did Stephen defeat Saul in synagogue debates? (6:8-12)
    D) Saul disagreed with his rabbi Gamaliel
    E) many Hellenistic Jewish believers fled including Philip (another of the 7 deacons)
    F) Philip preached Christ as he fled (Samaria, Ethiopian Eunuch, etc)
    G) Philip eventually settled in Caesarea (public enemy #1?)

2) Saul the Persecutor (vs 1-2)
    A) Saul-still leading the persecution against Hellenistic Jewish Christians
    B) he sought & received authority from the high priest to arrest Christians (male & female) in Damascus & return them to Jerusalem for trial (Ac 26:11)
    C) synagogues-meeting places for Jews to study the Old Testament (led by a rabbi)
    D) Damascus-140 miles NE of Jerusalem (large Jewish population)
    E) Saul-a Pharisee/rabbi working with Sadducees/priests
    F) the Way-ancient name for Christianity (Jesus is the way of salvation; Jn 14:6)
    G) since 6AD the high priest had the right to bring religious violators back to Jerusalem

3) Jesus Appears to Saul (vs 3-6) Acts 22:6-21; 26:12-18
    A) near Damascus Saul was confronted by a bright light & he fell to the ground
    B) he heard a voice-"Why are you persecuting Me?"
    C) Saul asked, "who are you Lord?" (Yahweh or Master?)

D) the speaker identified Himself as Jesus (1 Cor 15:8)

    1)whom you are persecuting-Mt 25:40, 45; 1 Jn 4:20-21

    2) hard to kick against the goads (a pointed rod used to urge an animal-divine persuasion)

E) Saul-trembling & astonished (fear & shock)

F) "Lord what do you want me to do?"

G) go into Damascus & you'll be told what to do

4) <u>Saul was Blinded by the Light</u> (vs 7-9)

A) the men traveling with him stood speechless

    1) possibly temple police

    2) they heard a voice, but saw no one (see 22:9)

    3) they had been knocked down, but got up before Saul did (see 26:14)

B) Saul arose from the ground; he was blind

C) the others led him by the hand into Damascus

D) Saul was without sight for 3 days; he didn't eat or drink

    -3 days to think about his spiritual blindness-Jn 9:39-41

E) Saul received more visits from Jesus (Gal 1:1, 15-18; 1 Cor 11:23; Ac 22:17-21)

F) Saul's conversion is evidence for Christ's resurrection

    -1 Tm 1:15; 1 Cor 15:9 (also Peter & James)

5) <u>Conclusion-the Power of Jesus to Change Lives</u>

A) Rm 1:16; 6:14, 17-18; Eph 1:19-20; 1 Cor 4:20

B) Eph 2:8-9; Paul is an example of salvation by grace

    1) the persecutor became the persecuted

    2) the hater of Christians became the lover of Christians

    3) evangelist, apologist, church-planter, author, pastor, theologian, missionary, & martyr

C) no sin is so great that our Savior cannot forgive

D) Jesus saves & changes lives

God Sends Ananias to Saul (Acts 9:10-22)

1) <u>Introduction</u>
    A) Saul led the persecution of the Hellenistic Jewish
        Christians
    B) he got written authorization from the high priest to arrest
        Christians in the synagogues in Damascus & return
        them to Jerusalem to stand trial before the Sanhedrin
    C) on the road to Damascus, Jesus appeared to Saul & saved
        him (Saul is blinded & does not eat for 3 days)

2) <u>God Commands Ananias to Heal Saul</u> (vs 10-16)
    A) Ananias - a disciple living in Damascus (10-12)
    B) the Lord appeared to him in a vision
    C) the Lord's orders for Ananias
        1) go to a street called Straight (still exists today)
        2) go to the house of Judas
        3) Saul of Tarsus is there praying
        4) the Lord has already given Saul a vision of Ananias
            restoring Saul's sight
    D) Ananias' initial response (13-14)
        1) he had heard about Saul's persecution of Christians
            in Jerusalem
        2) he also heard that Saul had received authority from
            the chief priests to persecute Christians in
            Damascus
        3) saints = (hagiois) those set apart for God's purposes
        4) all who call on your name (Joel 2:32)
        5) paraphrase - "Lord, are you sure you're sending me
            to the right guy?" (like Jonah & Nineveh)
    E) the Lord's response to Ananias (15-16)
        1) go (I know what I'm doing)

2) Saul is my chosen vessel (God decides whom He
    will use)
3) to bear My name before:
    a) Gentiles (Paul was the apostle to the Gentiles)
    b) kings (Paul eventually preached to Caesar)
    c) the children of Israel (he always preached in
        synagogues first)
4) Saul will suffer much for the cause of Christ
    -shipwrecked, stoned, scourged, imprisonments,
        beheaded
5) paraphrase - "Ananias, I know what I'm doing"

3) <u>Ananias Heals & Baptizes Saul</u> (vs 17-19)
    A) Ananias was puzzled by the Lord's orders for him
    B) but, he obeyed
    C) he may not have agreed with God . . . but, he obeyed
    D) Ananias, through the power of God, healed Saul
    E) scales fell from Saul's eyes
    F) laying on of hands (symbolizes serious intercession)
    G) Saul was filled with the Holy Spirit
        -distinction between filling & indwelling
    H) Saul was water baptized (no year long course needed)
    I) Saul had come to Damascus to kill Ananias (& others)
    J) now Ananias heals Paul
    K) Saul ate for the first time in 3 days & was strengthened
    L) Saul spent some days in Damascus fellowshipping with
        the disciples he intended to kill

4) <u>Saul Preaches in Damascus</u> (vs 20-22)
    A) immediately (Saul was ready to be used of God)
    B) Saul preached in the synagogues in Damascus

C) many synagogues, but only one temple

D) Saul preached Jesus in the synagogues he intended to attack & disrupt

E) the Christ = Jesus is the Jewish Messiah, the one God anointed to rescue Israel

F) the Son of God = Jesus is God; He is one in nature with the Father

G) Saul's listeners were amazed-the one who came to destroy the church is now teaching the church & leading others to Christ (God turned Saul around)

H) Saul increased in strength (physical & spiritual)

I) Saul, like Stephen had done, refuted the Jews in debate in the synagogues & proved that Jesus is the Jewish Messiah

5) Conclusion

A) are we, like Ananias, willing to obey God even when it hurts? (John 14:15)

B) are we, like Ananias, wiling to forgive our enemies? (Ephesians 4:32; Matthew 6:14-15)

C) be an Ananias--obey God & forgive others

D) are we, like Saul, willing to suffer greatly for Jesus?

E) are we, like Saul, willing to turn around, admit we were wrong & proclaim God's truth & proclaim Jesus? (Matthew 10:32-33)

F) are people amazed at the changes God has made in our lives? (is God glorified by your testimony?)

H) are you willing to share Jesus with others, even if they debate you?

I) be a Saul/Paul--let Jesus change you, be willing to suffer for Jesus, share Jesus with others

Paul Preaches In Damascus & Jerusalem
(Acts 9:23-31)

1) Introduction
   - after Saul's conversion, he preached in the synagogues in Damascus, proving that Jesus is the Jewish Messiah

2) Saul Escapes Damascus (23-25)
   - A) the Jews in Damascus plotted to kill Saul (23)
      - 1) 2 Corinthians 11:32-33
         - a) Arabia - southeast of Damascus; as far west as the Red Sea
         - b) King Aretas IV of Arabia (Nabatea)
         - c) he lived from 9BC to 40AD
         - d) he was the father-in-law of Herod Antipas
         - e) Damascus was often considered under the jurisdiction of Arabia
         - f) the governor of Damascus wanted Saul dead; he received many complaints from the Jews living there
   - B) Saul is rescued by believers through a house in the city wall (24-25)
   - C) Saul had preached 3 years in Damascus & Arabia following his conversion (Galatians 1:15-18)

3) Saul Preaches in Jerusalem (26-29)
   - A) Saul came to Jerusalem
   - B) the disciples were afraid of him
      - 1) it's not easy to change your reputation
      - 2) the disciples thought he was a spy in their midst
   - C) Barnabas defended Saul before the disciples
      - 1) Barnabas = son of encouragement-Ac 4:36-37; 13:2
      - 2) Barnabas told the disciples about Saul's conversion & preaching ministry in Damascus

D) the disciples accepted Saul as a brother due to Barnabas'
intercession

E) Saul preached to the Hellenists in Jerusalem
1) Hellenists = Greek-speaking Jews
2) they were Saul's former associates
3) Saul picked up where Stephen left off (Acts 6:8-10)

F) the Hellenists (Saul's former associates) wanted to kill
Saul

4) <u>Saul Sent to Tarsus</u> (30)
A) the believers rescued Saul
1) they brought him to Caesarea (50 miles north of
Jerusalem)
2) they shipped him to Tarsus (Saul's birthplace)
a) about 300 miles north of Jerusalem
b) the leading city of the region of Cilicia
c) had several schools of philosophy, rhetoric, law
3) Galatians 1:18-21

5) <u>The Church at Peace</u> (31)

6) <u>Conclusion</u>
A) <u>Saul's Commitment to Christ (his work ethic)</u>
(1 Corinthians 15:9-10)
1) he remembers where he came from (saved by grace)
2) he gives God all the glory (empowered by grace)
3) he gave 100% of himself to the Lord's service
a) Galatians 6:9-10; Ephesians 5:15-16
b) Colossians 3:23-24; 4:5-6
c) Philippians 3:12-14; 4:13
4) he spoke boldly about Jesus (Acts 9:30; 4:31)
5) he fulfilled God's mission for his life (2 Timothy 4:7)
B) <u>Barnabas' Encouragement of Other Believers</u>
-do we come alongside sincere new believers who are
judged by other Christians due to their past sins?

The Early Church Enjoys Peace & Growth
(Acts 9:31)

1) Introduction
   A) Saul, the main persecutor of the church, was converted on the road to Damascus
   B) 3 years after his conversion he preached in Jerusalem
   C) he was forced to flee to Tarsus due to persecution
2) The Church in Palestine Enjoys Peace & Growth (9:31)
   A) Judea, Galilee, Samaria (Palestine-the land of Israel)
   B) peace (eirene; freedom from hostility)
      1) religious freedom/lack of severe persecution
      2) Roman Emperor Tiberius died
      3) new Emperor Caligula wanted to build a statue of himself in the Jewish temple
      4) the attention of the Jewish religious leaders was diverted (they no longer focused on believers)
      5) the church grew & served Jesus regardless of whether times were good (peace) or bad (persecution)
      6) peace provides opportunity for service
      7) John 9:4; Matthew 9:37-38
   C) edified (oikodomeo; built up; to build a house)
      1) spiritual growth & maturity was promoted
      2) the character of believers was developed
      3) Ephesians 4:11-15
      4) no edification without discipleship
      5) edification is a requirement for service (gas-car)
   D) walking in the fear of the Lord (phobos)
      1) Proverbs 1:7; Philippians 2:12-13 (awe, respect, fear)
      2) we must never forget we work for God

        3) Moses personally knew God, but still had to take his
            sandals off when he stood on holy ground
        4) the early church remembered Ananias & Sapphira
        5) serving Jesus is not a game
        6) the fear of the Lord is a <u>motivation for service</u>
  E) <u>walking in the comfort of the Holy Spirit</u>
        1) comfort (paraklesei; the act of coming alongside
            another to comfort & defend them)
        2) God is our comfort (2 Corinthians 1:3-4)
        3) fear-God is totally just; comfort-God is love
        4) the Holy Spirit is always with us
        5) Jesus is always with us (Mt 28:19-20; Hb 13:5)
        6) comfort is both <u>an empowerment for service</u> &
            <u>a reward for service</u>
  F) <u>the churches multiplied</u>
        1) new converts were added; the churches grew
        2) multiplication is often <u>a result of service</u>
3) <u>Conclusion</u>
  A) if we want our churches to grow, we must have the
     following qualities:
        1) <u>we must edify our people </u>(disciple them; build them
            up; prepare them for service)
        2) <u>we must have the proper fear/respect of the Lord</u>
          -Christianity is not a social club
        3) <u>we must accept the Holy Spirit's comfort</u> (Jn 16:33)
  B) we are experiencing a time of peace (lack of severe
     persecution)
  C) we must make the most of our opportunities & take
     advantage of our religious freedom (while we still have
     it); we must not get complacent or apathetic

Peter's Miracles & Ministry in Judea
(Acts 9:32-43)

1) <u>Introduction</u>
     A) Peter takes advantage of the temporary relief from persecution
     B) he leaves Jerusalem & preached throughout Judea
     C) the saints in Lydda & Joppa
          1) possibly converts from Philip's ministry
          2) possibly Jerusalem saints who fled during Saul's persecution

2) <u>Peter Heals a Paralyzed Man in Lydda</u> (vs 32-35)
     A) Peter preached throughout Judean region
     B) he visited the saints in Lydda
          1) saints = hagious (separated ones; living, not dead)
          2) Lydda - about 25 miles NW of Jerusalem
     C) Aeneas - paralyzed & bedridden for 8 years
     D) Peter - "Jesus the Christ heals you"
          1) Jesus = Jewish Messiah (deliverer of Israel)
          2) Peter gave the credit & glory to Jesus
          3) it was Jesus' healing power, not Peter's
          4) Peter healed Aeneas; this led many to believe

3) <u>Peter Raises Tabitha from the Dead in Joppa</u> (vs 36-42)
     A) Joppa - about 12 miles NW of Lydda & 37 miles NW of Jerusalem; on Mediterranean Coast
     B) Tabitha/Dorcas died
          1) she had lived a life of service
          2) she had made garments for poor widows
          3) upon her death, the disciples sent for Peter
          4) the widows she had helped wept greatly for her

        5) Peter had the widows leave the room (Mt 9:23-25)

        6) Peter said "Tabitha arise" (Mark 5:37-42)

        7) Peter raised her from the dead

   C) because of this miracle, many more believed

4) <u>The Signs of an Apostle</u> (2 Corinthians 12:12)

   A) God confirmed the initial preaching of His Word with great signs & wonders

   B) Moses & Jesus & the apostles (Ac 7:36; Hb 2:3-4)

5) <u>Peter Stayed Many Days in Joppa with Simon the Tanner</u> (vs 43)

   A) tanners were social outcasts in Israel

   B) they were considered "unclean" since they worked with skins of dead animals (this violated Old Testament ceremonial laws - Lev 11:40)

   C) tanners made animal hides into leather

   D) God was already teaching Peter a lesson

   E) 1 Tm 4:1-5; Ac 10 (if God declares something clean, it is clean/Gentiles, previously forbidden food)

   F) when we serve God, He often takes us out of our comfort zone (even during times free from persecution)

6) <u>Conclusion</u>

   A) Jesus' power was & still is at work (Rm 1:16; 1 Cor 4:20)

   B) many were coming to Christ for salvation

   C) God was preparing Peter's heart for his future ministry with "unclean" Gentiles (Ac 10; Cornelius)

   D) will you choose a life of comfort or a life of service?

   E) is Jesus' power at work in your life?

   F) without Jesus' power displayed in your life, the lost will not come to Christ

The Gospel Spreads to the Gentiles
(Parts 1 &2; Acts 10:1-16)

1) Introduction
   A) Peter left Jerusalem & ministered in Judea
   B) he healed Aeneas & raised Dorcas from the dead
   C) he was staying at the home of Simon the tanner in Joppa
   D) God was working on Peter's heart & taking him out of his
      comfort zone

2) Cornelius sends for Peter (vs 1-8)
   A) Caesarea (about 30 miles north of Joppa; capital of Judea
      under Roman procurators; a strong Gentile presence)
   B) Cornelius
      1) centurion - Roman official who led 100 Roman
         soldiers
      2) Italian Regiment/cohort - about 1,000 soldiers
      3) a devout man
      4) one who feared God (he worshiped the God of Israel)
      5) with all his household (he was influential)
      6) generous; helped the needy
      7) a prayer warrior
      8) he was a Gentile; not circumcised (not a full convert)
      9) not saved, but seeking God (Ac 11:14, 18; Jer 29:13;
         Mt 23:37; 2 Pt 3:9; Jn 3:19-21; Hb 11:6)
   C) Cornelius' vision
      1) the ninth hour of the day (3pm-one of the times of
         Jewish prayer; Ac 3:1; 9am/3pm/sunset)
      2) an angel of God came to him in a vision
      3) God accepted his prayers & donations (Jm 4:8)
      4) told to send men to Joppa for Simon Peter

        5) he's staying at Simon the tanner's house

        6) Simon Peter will tell you what you must do

    D) Cornelius' Response

        1) he selected 2 of his servants & a devout soldier

        2) he sent them to Joppa for Peter

3) Peter's Vision (vs 9-16) {Part 2}

    A) God prepares Peter for ministry to the Gentiles

    B) the keys to the Kingdom (Mt 16:13-19)

        -Jews (Ac 2); Samaritans (Ac 8); Gentiles (Ac 10)

    C) Peter prays on the roof at noon (the 6th hour-the next day)

    D) Peter was hungry, but fell into a trance

    E) his vision

        1) something like a sheet is lowered down to him

        2) in it were all kinds of animals

        3) he is told to "rise, kill, & eat"

        4) Peter's response - "I have never eaten anything
            common or unclean"

        5) "what God has cleansed you must not call common"

        6) God repeated the vision 3 times to break down
            Peter's prejudices

    F) his lesson

        1) Old Testament shadows no longer apply; they were
            fulfilled by Christ (Col 2:16-17; Jn 4:19-24)

        2) Jewish dietary laws no longer apply (Lev 11)

        3) often, we must be taken out of our comfort zone to
            be ready to move with God

        4) God desires the salvation of all; the Gospel is not
            limited to Israel (Isa 45:22)

        5) God is preparing Peter to preach to the Gentiles

The Gospel Spreads to the Gentiles
(Parts 3 & 4; Acts 10:17-35)

1) Introduction
    A) Cornelius' vision about Simon Peter
    B) Peter's vision about "unclean" food

2) Messengers from Cornelius Find Peter (vs 17-23)
    A) God-fearer (Prov 1:7; 2:1-6)
    B) Peter invited Gentiles to stay with him
        1) even a despised Roman soldier
        2) Peter was changed due to the vision
        3) do we love all people?
    C) Peter left for Caesarea to meet Cornelius
        -he took 6 Jewish believers with him (Ac 11:12)

3) Peter Meets with Cornelius (vs 24-33)
    A) Cornelius had gathered his friends & relatives to hear
        Peter (Cornelius was very respected)
    B) Peter refused to accept worship (Ex 20:1-6; Rv 19:10)
        1) Roman Catholic popes
        2) do we give God all the glory?
        3) are we building God's Kingdom or our own?
    C) Jews believed they would be ceremonially unclean if they
        entered a Gentile's house (Jn 18:28-29)
    D) Jesus is our peace; He has broken down every wall
        1) no distinction in church between Jews & Gentiles
        2) Eph 2:11-19; Gal 3:28

4) <u>Peter Begins His Message</u> (34-35)
    A) God shows no partiality (God loves all mankind)
       1) Rm 2:9-12; 3:20-24; 11:32; Gal 3:28
       2) God desires all to be saved (2 Pt 3:9; 1 Tm 2:1-6)
       3) Jesus commands us to preach to all people
          (Mt 28:19-20; Ac 1:8; Isa 45:22)
    B) God-seekers will find Jesus (Jn 3:19-21; Jer 29:13)
       1) God-seekers not saved until they come to Jesus
          (Ac 11:14)
       2) God draws all men to Himself (Jn 12:32; 16:7-11)
          -lesser lights of creation & conscience (Rm 1, 2)
       3) God is near to all who call on Him in truth
          (Ps 145:18-19; Jm 4:8)
       4) God is in control (sovereign; Rm 10:14-15)

5) <u>Conclusion</u>
    A) do we love all people & long to see them saved?
    B) do we really appreciate our unity in Christ?
    C) do we seek God with all our hearts?
    D) do we allow our religious traditions get between us &
       Jesus?
    E) are we building God's Kingdom or our own?
    F) do we give God all the glory?
    G) do we acknowledge that our God is in control?

The Gospel Spreads to the Gentiles
(Parts 5 & 6; Acts 10:34-43)

1) <u>Introduction</u>
    A) Cornelius' vision; Peter's vision
    B) Peter shares the gospel with Cornelius' household
    C) Cornelius & his household are Gentiles

2) <u>Peter's Sermon</u> (vs 34-43)
    A) God's Word is proclaimed in Israel & now needs to be
        proclaimed throughout the world (peace through Jesus)
    B) <u>Jesus is Lord of all</u> (34-36) {Jesus is God/Yahweh}
        1) God shows no favoritism; He loves all people
            (vs 34-35; Jn 3:16; 2 Pt 3:9)
        2) God sent His Word to Israel (36)
            -the gospel (Peter gives outline of the future
                gospels?)
        3) His Word deals with peace through Jesus
            a) peace with God (Rm 5:1)
            b) peace among men (Eph 2:13-18)
            c) Christ = Jesus is the Jewish Messiah
        4) Jesus is Lord of all (both Jew & Gentile; Rm 10:12)
    C) <u>Jesus' Ministry</u> (vs 37-38)
        1) began in Galilee (Jesus came from Galilee)
        2) John's baptism-the start of Jesus' public ministry
            (Mt 3:1, 13-17)
        3) Jesus' ministry spread throughout Judea
        4) God anointed (Christ = anointed One) Jesus with
            Holy Spirit & power at His baptism (prepared
            Him for His ministry/healing, exorcisms)

        5) Jesus was declared to be the Messiah at His baptism
            (Jn 1:33-34)
        6) God was with Jesus (Jn 14:8-11)
D) <u>Jesus' death & resurrection</u> (vs 39-41)
        1) we are witnesses of these things
        2) Jesus was crucified by men (rejected)
        3) Jesus was raised by God (exalted)
        4) Jesus appeared to eye-witnesses & proved He was
            alive (Acts 1:3; 1 Cor 15:3-8; Lk 24)
E) <u>the Great Commission</u> (vs 42)
        -Jesus commanded the apostles to preach to the
            people (Mt 28:19-20; Ac 1:8)
F) <u>salvation through Jesus</u> (vs 42-44)
        1) God ordained Jesus to be the judge of the living &
            the dead (our eternal destinies rest in His hands)
        2) all the prophets testify of Jesus & His salvation
            (Jn 5:39-40; Lk 24:25-27)
        3) whoever (Jew or Gentile) believes in Jesus will have
            their sins forgiven

3) <u>Conclusion</u>
    A) Peter was prepared to share the gospel (are we?)
    B) the gospel includes Jesus' deity, death, resurrection,
        ministry, & salvation
    C) the Great Commission applies to us

The Gospel Spreads to the Gentiles
(Part 7; Acts 10:44-48)

1) Introduction
  A) Peter preaches the gospel to Gentiles
  B) Cornelius & friends

2) The Holy Spirit Baptizes Peter's Listeners (vs 44)
  A) salvation is through faith alone (Acts 10:43; Jn 3:16; 6:47)
  B) water baptism is not essential to salvation
  C) the Gentiles share in Pentecost (Acts 2)
  D) 1 Corinthians 12:13

3) The Jewish Believers were Amazed (vs 45)
  A) they thought Gentiles could only be saved if they became
      Jews (circumcision, O. T. law, plus Jesus-Acts 15:1)
  B) the Holy Spirit only baptizes those He regenerates

4) Evidence of Baptism with the Holy Spirit (vs 46)
  A) spoke with tongues & exalted God (Acts 2:1-4)
  B) Peter & his friends needed evidence of the Gentiles'
      salvation & baptism with the Holy Spirit
  C) one body, one church (both Jew & Gentile)
  D) 1 Corinthians 12:13; 29-31
  E) not everyone has the gift of tongues
  F) fruit of the Spirit is evidence of Spirit baptism today
  G) Galatians 5:22-23
  H) it was important that God provide clear, miraculous
      evidence for the Jewish church that Gentiles could be
      saved by Jesus without converting to Judaism

5) <u>Peter Tells His Colleagues to Baptize the Converts</u> (vs 47-48)
- A) these Gentiles (Cornelius & his friends) received the Holy Spirit the same way the Jews did
- B) this was evidence of their salvation & Spirit baptism
- C) there was no reason to withhold baptism from them (Acts 11:17; 15:7-11)
- D) Peter ordered them to be baptized, but not circumcised
- E) Romans 2:28-29 (true circumcision is of the heart)
- F) indwelling vs. filling of the Holy Spirit
- G) Spirit Baptism is the initial filling with the Holy Spirit
- H) it now occurs at regeneration/conversion
- I) Acts was a transitional period
- J) Cornelius asked them to stay a few days

6) <u>Conclusion</u>
- A) salvation is by God's grace alone through Faith alone in Jesus alone (Ephesians 2:8-9; John 3:16-18)
- B) God saves both Jew & Gentile solely through faith in Jesus, not through the Old Testament Law
- C) water baptism is not essential to salvation, though we do it out of obedience to Christ (Matthew 28:19-20)
- D) the Holy Spirit distributes the gifts of the Spirit as He wills (seek the fruit of the Spirit; 1 Corinthians 12:11; Galatians 5:22-23)
- E) Jew & Gentile form one body in the church
- F) God has no favorites; He desires to save all people

Peter Defends Salvation by Grace
(Acts 11:1-18)

1) Introduction
- A) Peter led Cornelius & other Gentiles to Jesus
- B) he spent time at the Gentile's house
- C) word got back to the Jewish believers in Judea

2) Peter's Actions are Called into Question (vs 1-3)
- A) the apostles
- B) the brothers (other Jewish believers in Judea)
- C) heard that the Gentiles had received Jesus
- D) "those of the circumcision" (see Gal 2:11-12)
   - 1) Jewish Christians who believed that Gentiles had to become Jews when they became Christians
   - 2) they wanted Gentiles to be circumcised & obey the Law of Moses
   - 3) they frowned upon fellowship between Jews & Gentiles, & the eating of Gentile food
- E) different Jewish-Christian perspectives
   - 1) Paul (become all things to all men; 1 Cor 9:19-23)
   - 2) James (Jewish Christians still need to obey Law of Moses, but not Gentiles; weaker brother?)
   - 3) "the circumcision" believed that Gentiles had to become Jews to be saved by Jesus (Ac 15:1)

3) Peter Defends God's Grace (vs 4-17)
- A) Peter explains his actions
   - 1) Peter's vision-all food is clean (4-10)
   - 2) 3 visitors from Cornelius (11)
   - 3) Peter & 6 Jewish Christians meet with Cornelius (12)
   - 4) an angel told Cornelius that Peter would tell him & his household the salvation message (13-14)

        5) the Holy Spirit baptized the Gentiles while Peter
            spoke to them (15-16) {just like Pentecost}
        6) the Gentiles received the same gift as the Jews (17)
            A) faith in Jesus was the only condition
            B) Peter could not restrain God; he could not
                prevent God from doing what God chose to
                do (God is in charge, not Peter)
      B) Gentiles can be saved through faith in Jesus without
          circumcision or the Old Testament Law (Eph 2:8-9)
      C) Gentiles are not 2nd class Christians (Spirit Baptism)

4) <u>Peter's Listeners Accept His Argument</u> (vs 18)
      A) there were silenced (they had no comeback)
      B) they glorified God
      C) they acknowledged that God gave eternal life to Gentiles
          solely through faith in Jesus
      D) faith = turn to Jesus (trust in Jesus for salvation)
      E) repentance = turn from sin
      F) this issue will resurface at the Jerusalem Council (Ac 15)

5) <u>Conclusion</u>
      A) salvation is not by the works of the law (Romans 3:20)
      B) salvation is by God's grace alone through faith alone in
          Jesus alone (Ephesians 2:8-9)
      C) the Law was a tutor to lead the Jews to Christ (Gal 3:24)
      D) Gentiles & Jews are equal in Christ (Eph 2:11-18)
      E) Gentiles are not second class Christians (Gal 3:26-28)

Antioch Becomes the Center for Gentile Christianity (Acts 11:19-30)

1) Introduction
    A) the Church was primarily Jewish & centered in Jerusalem
    B) few Gentile converts (Ethiopian Eunuch & Cornelius)
    C) now, more Gentiles come to Christ
2) The Gospel is Preached to Gentiles in Antioch (vs 19-21)
    A) the persecution of the Church after Stephen's martyrdom
        forced many believers to flee from Judea
    B) as they fled they preached the Gospel in Phoenicia,
        Cyprus, & Antioch (Acts 1:8)
    C) at first, they preached to Jews only (in the synagogues)
    D) but some Christians who were originally from Cyprus &
        Cyrene spoke to the Greeks (Gentiles) in Antioch
    E) they preached the Lord Jesus to the Gentiles & many of
        the Gentiles accepted Jesus
3) Barnabas & Paul Minister at Antioch (vs 22-26)
    A) news of the Gentile conversions got back to Jerusalem
    B) the apostles sent Barnabas to Antioch to investigate
        -Barnabas was from Cyprus (Ac 4:36)
    C) just as they sent Peter & John to Samaria (Acts 8)
        1) they were given the keys to the kingdom
        2) verified that the same Gospel was being preached
    D) Barnabas saw the grace of God (He saved the pagans)
    E) he rejoiced (compare with Jonah)
    F) he encouraged them to endure in Christ
    G) Barnabas = "Son of Encouragement" (Acts 4:36-37)
    H) he was full of the Holy Spirit & faith
    I) his encouragement led to more conversions
    J) he needed a helper in the ministry
    K) he traveled to Tarsus to find Saul

L) he brought Saul to Antioch (Acts 9:26-30)

M) he & Saul/Paul taught the believers in Antioch for a year

N) the disciples were first called "Christians" in Antioch

    1) before that called "the Way"

    2) considered a branch of Judaism

    3) now the Gentile church was considered by outsiders to be an entirely new religion

    4) Christ = anointed one (Messiah)

    5) to the pagan Gentiles, Christ was a proper name

4) <u>Antioch Believers Give to Judean Believers</u> (vs 27-30)

    A) prophets from Jerusalem would visit Antioch (unity)

    B) Agabus predicted a global famine was to come

    C) this happened in during the reign of Claudius Caesar (41-54AD; confirmed by secular history)

    D) the Gentile Christians of Antioch donated funds to help the Jerusalem church get through the famine

    E) they wanted to help the mother church

    F) they sent their donations to the Jerusalem church with Barnabas & Saul (one united church--Jew & Gentile)

    G) Paul never forgot the Jerusalem church (1 Cor 16:1-4)

5) <u>Conclusion</u>

    A) the Gospel spread to both Jew & Gentile/unity-one church

    C) we must encourage one another to persevere in the Faith

    D) we must rejoice when we see others get saved

    E) we must teach new converts

    F) we must take care of one another

    G) God will bring good out of our sufferings (persecution)

    H) God often takes us out of our comfort zone so that we can depend on Him & have new opportunities to serve Him

The Death of James, Son of Zebedee
(Acts 12:1-2)

1) Introduction
   - A) Hellenistic Jewish Christians were the first to be persecuted (they realized the temple had fulfilled its purpose)
   - B) about 41AD the apostles began to be targeted for persecution (they were now preaching to Gentiles)
   - C) the Jewish religious leaders hated the Gentiles more than they hated the gospel (jealousy; Romans 11:11)

2) Herod the King (vs 1)
   - A) Herod Agrippa I
   - B) the nephew of Herod Antipas (executed John the Baptist)
   - C) the grandson of Herod the Great (tried to kill baby Jesus)
   - D) Herod the Great was an Edomite (hated by the Jews)
   - E) Herod Agrippa I (his mother was Jewish-a Hasmonean queen, from the Maccabees-had waged guerilla warfare against Syria; some Jews accepted Herod Agrippa I)
   - F) in 41AD, the Roman Emperor Claudius gave Herod Agrippa I control over Judea (Jerusalem was there)
   - G) Herod Agrippa I desired to please the Jews; he was more popular with the Jews than his descendants were
   - H) about 44AD, he began to persecute the church to try to please the Jews

3) Herod executes James the Son of Zebedee (vs 2)
   - A) he singled out the apostles
   - B) the apostles were now preaching to the Gentiles
   - C) this was not popular with the Jews
   - D) now the apostles were targeted for persecution just as the Hellenistic Jewish Christians had been (Stephen, etc.)
   - E) Herod had James beheaded around 44AD

F) <u>so much potential . . . the life of James, Son of Zebedee</u>
    1) the elder brother of John, the beloved disciple
    2) one of the 12 apostles; a wealthy fisherman
    3) may have been a cousin of Jesus & a follower of
        John the Baptist (Salome-their mother?; Mt 27:56;
        Mk 15:40-41; 16:1; Jn 19:25; Jn 1:35-42)
    4) one of the first 4 apostles called by Jesus
        (Matthew 4:18-22)
    5) one of the "inner circle" of apostles (Peter, James, &
        John-only apostles present at the raising of Jairus'
daughter, the transfiguration, & Jesus' agony in
Gethsemane)
    6) Jesus nicknamed James & John the "sons of thunder"
    7) Luke 9:51-55; Mark 3:17
    8) he & his brother desired glory for themselves & were
        looking for a conquering, political Messiah
        (Mk 10:32-45)
    9) Jesus knew that James & John were willing to suffer
        & die for Him
    10) James was the first apostle to be martyred
        a) why did God allow him to die so early in his
          ministry?
        b) he had so much potential . . . but no regrets
        c) he was willing to both live for Jesus & die for
          Jesus-Jesus was His life
4) <u>Conclusion</u>-Mk 8:34-36; 2 Corinthians 5:15
    A) are you willing to carry your cross?
    B) are you willing to deny self?
    C) are you willing to live for Jesus?
    D) are you willing to die for Jesus?

Peter Miraculously Set Free; Herod Dies
(Acts 12:1-25)

1) Introduction
    A) as the Gospel began to be spread to the Gentiles, the
        apostles became the primary targets for persecution
    B) Herod Agrippa I had James the Son of Zebedee beheaded
    C) In an attempt to please the Jewish religious leaders he also
        had Peter arrested & planned to kill him after the feast
        days had been completed

2) Herod Agrippa I Arrests Peter (vs 1-4)
    A) Herod kills James & arrests Peter
    B) Days of Unleavened Bread-considered part of the
        Passover Feast (religious tradition more important than
        Jesus or justice)
    C) 4 squads of soldiers guarded Peter (16 soldiers in all)
    D) to prevent an escape

3) An Angel Sets Peter Free (vs 5-17)
    A) Peter was imprisoned
    B) constant prayer was offered for him by believers
    C) Jm 5:16-18; Lk 18:1-8
    D) Peter was chained between 2 soldiers
        1) 2 soldiers probably guarded the door
        2) 4 other soldiers stayed awake; 8 soldiers slept
    E) sometimes we don't expect God to answer our prayers
        -Jews believed in guardian angels (Mt 18:10)
    F) John Mark later became the author of *The Gospel of Mark*

4) <u>Peter Leaves Jerusalem</u> (vs 17)
    A) Peter, James (Jesus' half-brother), & John had led the
        Jerusalem church up to this point (Gal 1:18-19; 2:9)
    B) the original apostles now had to flee Jerusalem
    C) James (Jesus' half-brother) now became the sole leader of
        the Jerusalem church
    D) did Peter immediately go to Rome? Or, did he go to
        Antioch (Gal 2:11-14)?

5) <u>God Punishes Herod Agrippa I</u> (vs 18-24)
    A) Herod Agrippa I executed the Roman soldiers (18-19)
    B) he then went to Caesarea (the official Roman capitol of
        the region)
    C) the people of Tyre & Sidon were dependent upon Herod
        for food (20)
    D) they praised Herod & called him a god (21-22)
        -helping the poor is church's job, not government's
    E) Herod accepted their praise & refused to give the glory to
        God (23)
    F) he was eaten by worms & died
    G) Herod's death was also recorded by Josephus (though
        Josephus doesn't mention the worms & adds that it took
        Herod 5 days to die while having horrible internal pain)
    H) Herod died, but the Gospel spread & the church grew
    I) Tertullian wrote "The blood of the martyrs is the seed of
        the church."

6) <u>Paul & Barnabas Return to Antioch</u> (vs 25)
    A) Paul & Barnabas had been in Jerusalem to deliver the
        Gentile donations (Acts 11:27-30)
    B) now they return to Antioch
    C) they take with them a young man named John Mark
        -he would accompany them on their first missionary
          journey & later write *The Gospel of Mark*

7) <u>Conclusion</u>
    A) are we willing, like James & Peter, to suffer for Jesus?
    B) Joshua 1:9
    C) is religious tradition more important to us than Jesus or
        justice?
    D) do we earnestly & constantly pray?
    E) do we expect God to answer our prayers?
    F) do we. like Herod, seek the praise of men? (Gal 1:10)
    G) or, do we give God the glory
    H) Eph 2:8-9; 2 Cor 10:17; Jm 4:10

Paul & Barnabas Start Their First Missionary Journey (Acts 13:1-5)

1) Introduction (Acts 12 overview)
    A) Paul & Barnabas bring Antioch church's donations to
        Jerusalem church during a famine
    B) James (son of Zebedee) is beheaded by Herod
    C) Peter is imprisoned, but miraculously released
    D) God strikes King Herod dead
    E) Paul & Barnabas (& John Mark) return to Antioch (12:25)

2) Antioch Church Sends out Paul & Barnabas (vs 1-3)
    A) prophets & teachers in Antioch Church (vs 1)
        1) prophets = proclaimed God's truth
        2) teachers = instructed people in God's Word
        3) Barnabas & Paul (Saul)
        4) Simeon called Niger (African)
        5) Lucius of Cyrene (northern Africa)
        6) Manaen (he was raised with Herod the tetrarch)
            A) raised in royal court with Herod Antipas,
                youngest son of Herod the Great
            B) executed John the Baptist & tried Jesus
    B) as they served (worshiped) the Lord & fasted, the Holy
        Spirit spoke to them (vs 2)
        1) God often speaks to us when we worship Him
        2) fasting can help us to focus on God (deny flesh)
        3) Bible saints often fasted when they sought a word
            from God
        4) separate Paul & Barnabas for God's work to which
            they were called
        5) make sure God called you before you start a major
            task for Him

C) the prophets fasted & prayed again (vs 3)
    1) to empower & set apart Paul & Barnabas
    2) they laid hands on them (anointed them for God's
       work) & sent them away

3) <u>Paul & Barnabas Begin Their First Missionary Journey</u> (4-5)
    A) they were sent by the Holy Spirit
    B) they went to Selucia (a few miles south of Antioch)
    C) from there they sailed to the Island of Cyprus (an island to
       the southeast of Antioch)
    D) Salamis was a city is eastern Cyprus
    E) Paul & Barnabas preached the Word first in the
       synagogues (to Jews, converts, & God-fearers)
    F) Paul's strategy - synagogues, then marketplaces (Rm 1:16)
    G) John Mark was with them as their assistant

4) <u>They Will Witness to a Government Official & Confront a
    Sorcerer</u> (vs 6-12)

5) <u>Conclusion-Application</u>
    A) God speaks to us
       1) are we listening? (pray, fast, worship, study Word)
       2) *Experiencing God* by Blackaby & King
          -"God speaks by the Holy Spirit through the
          Bible, prayer, circumstances, & the church to
          reveal Himself, His purposes, and His ways."
    B) God wants to lead us (Prov 3:5-6)
    C) God wants to send us
       -harvest is plentiful, but workers are few (Mt 9:36-38)
    D) God wants to empower us (Jn 15:5; Eph 6:10-18)

Paul & Barnabas Confront a Sorcerer
(Acts 13:6-12)

1) Introduction
    A) Paul & Barnabas are commissioned by the Antioch church
        to begin their first missionary journey
    B) they went throughout the Island of Cyprus preaching in
        the synagogues
2) Bar-Jesus the Sorcerer (vs 6)
    A) Paphos was the Capital of Cyprus, nearly 100 miles west
        of Salamis
    B) it was a center of Aphrodite (Venus) worship
        1) the goddess of love, beauty, & fertility
        2) promoted sexual immorality & occultism
    C) Bar-Jesus = son of Jesus (or Joshua)
        1) sorcerer = magician, occultist (Greek word is magos)
        2) false prophet (claimed to speak for God; Mt 7:15)
        3) Jewish (was he claiming to be a representative of the
           real Jesus?; Acts 2?)
        4) also called Elymas the Sorcerer (Aramaic or Semitic
           word for sorcerer)
3) Sergius Paulus (vs 7)
    A) the proconsul (Roman official who governed Cyprus)
    B) an intelligent man = a wise leader, well-read?
    C) he probably heard of Paul & Barnabas' preaching
    D) he sent for them to hear the gospel
4) Bar-Jesus Opposes Paul & Barnabas (vs 8)
    A) also called Elymas the Sorcerer
    B) he wanted to prevent the proconsul from accepting Christ
    C) he was probably one of Sergius Paulus' personal advisors
    D) he didn't want to lose his job

5) <u>Paul Strikes Bar-Jesus with Blindness</u> (vs 9-11)

    A) Saul (Hebrew name) also called Paul

        1) Paul was his Roman name from birth

        2) now used for his ministry to the Gentiles

    B) filled with the Holy Spirit

        1) under the Holy Spirit's control

        2) absolute dependence on God

        3) the full armor of God (Eph 6:10-18)

    C) looked intently at Bar-Jesus

    D) accused him of deception & fraud

        1) not a true servant of God

        2) he was actually a son of the devil (Jn 8:42-44;

            Rev 2:8-9; 2 Cor 11:13-15)

        3) he was an enemy of righteousness (Rm 6:17-18)

        4) he was perverting the straight ways of the Lord

    E) the Lord strikes Bar-Jesus with temporary blindness

        1) Paul pronounces judgment on him (a warning)

        2) Paul also suffered temporary blindness after meeting

            Christ on the Road to Damascus (Ac 9)

    F) Bar-Jesus a false guide/false leader now had to be led by

        the hand (he who claimed he had spiritual insight was

        now rendered physically blind-Jn 9:39-41)

6) <u>The Proconsul Accepts Christ</u> (vs 12)

    --he is amazed at the power of God & acepts Christ

7) <u>Conclusion</u>

    A) we have access to the power of the Kingdom of God

    B) 1 Cor 4:20; Rm 1:16; 1 Jn 4:4; Eph 1:19-20

    C) power encounters of the Bible (1 Kings 18:21-24;

        Ex 7:10-12; Ac 8; Ac 16; Lk 8)

    D) we must acknowledge our absolute dependence on the

        Lord (Jn 15:5; Jude 9; Eph 6:10-18)

Spiritual Battle in the 21st Century

1) we have access to the power of the Kingdom of God
    (1 Cor 4:20; Rm 1:16; 1 Jn 4:4; Eph 1:19-20)
2) power encounters of the Bible
    (1 Kn 18:21-24; Ex 7:10-12; Ac 8; Ac 16; Lk 8)
3) we must acknowledge our absolute dependence on the Lord
    A) John 15:5
    B) Jude 9
    C) The Full Armor of God (Ephesians 6:10-18)
        1) be strong in God's power (not our own)
        2) our battle is spiritual (not physical)
        3) the full armor of God
            a) the belt of truth (sincerity; true beliefs)
            b) the breastplate of righteousness
                -faith plus love in action (Rm 14:23;
                    Jm 2:26; Mk 12:30-31; Rm 13:10)
            c) the shoes of the preparation of the gospel of
                peace (are you prepared to share your faith?)
            d) the shield of faith (trust in the Lord)
                -helps you defeat Satan's temptations
            e) the helmet of salvation (only believers can be
                prepared for spiritual battle)
            f) the sword of the Spirit (the Word of God)
                -our only offensive weapon (Ps 119:11)
                -we must be grounded in the Word (Mt 4)
            g) praying always in the Spirit
                -command & control (God is our source of
                strength)

Paul Preaches in Antioch of Pisidia (Acts 13:13-41)

Part 1 - *God Raised for Israel a Savior* (vs 13-25)

Part 2 - *God Raised the Savior for Israel* (vs 26-41)

1) Introduction (the start of Paul's first missionary journey)
    A) Island of Cyprus--Paul confronted Bar-Jesus
    B) led Sergius Paulus to Christ

2) Paul, Barnabas, & John Mark Sail from Paphos to Perga (13)
    A) Paphos-on the Island of Cyprus
    B) Perga-located on the south coast of Asia Minor (modern
        Turkey) in the region of Pamphylia
    C) John Mark returned to Jerusalem
    D) Acts 15:36-39; 2 Timothy 4:1; Gospel of Mark

3) Paul & Barnabas Visit a Synagogue in Antioch of Pisidia(14-15)
    A) not Antioch of Syria (the home church)
    B) Sabbath Day - Saturday (Jewish worship)
    C) elders read from Law & Prophets (Old Testament)
    D) elders asked Paul & Barnabas if they had a word of
        exhortation to share (parakleseos-called to the side of
        another to comfort & encourage them)

4) Paul Preaches a Sermon (vs 16-41)
    A) Part 1 - *God Raised for Israel a Savior* (vs 16-25)
        -Israel constantly falls, but God lifts her up
    B) he speaks to Jews & God-fearers (16)
        1) Men of Israel = the Jews
        2) God-fearers = Gentiles who believe the God of Israel
            is the one true God but have yet to be circumcised

C) <u>God exalted the Jews who were in bondage in Egypt</u> (17)
   -exalted = hupsosen (God raised her up; delivered her)
   -God chose the Israelite Fathers (Abraham, Isaac, etc.)
D) <u>God put up with His disobedient people</u> for 40 years in
   the wilderness (18)
E) <u>God gave the Jews the Promised Land-Canaan</u> (19)
   1) defeated 7 nations (Hittites, Gergashites, Amorites,
       Canaanites, Perizzites, Hivites, & Jebusites)
   2) land divided among 12 tribes
F) <u>Judges ruled until Samuel the Prophet</u> (20)
   1) 450 years of moral anarchy, sin, idolatry
   2) no king in Israel
   3) 13 Judges-Samson, Gideon, Deborah, Jephthah, etc.
   4) loose alliance of 12 tribes
   5) cycle of sin, bondage, repentance, deliverance
G) <u>Israel's first 2 Kings</u> (21-22)
   1) the people's choice-Saul (weak in faith; 40 more
       years of "wilderness wandering")
   2) God's choice-David (a man after God's own heart;
       the beginning of Israel's glorious years)
H) <u>the Son of David-the Messiah</u> (23)
   1) Jesus the Savior
   2) according to the Promise (the Messiah would come
       from the line of David-Jer 23:5-6; Isa 11:1;
       Ps 132:10-12; 2 Sam 7: 12-17)
I) <u>the Messiah's Forerunner</u> (24-25)
   1) John the Baptist
   2) baptized for the repentance of sin to prepare people
       for the coming Messiah
   3) John admitted he was not the Messiah
   4) he admitted the Messiah was infinitely greater than
       he was

5) <u>Conclusion of Part One of Paul's Sermon</u>
   A) Paul was asked to give a word of encouragement

B) throughout her history, Israel constantly fell, but God
    continually raised her up

C) eventually, God raised up for Israel a Savior, the Messiah,
    the Son of David

D) application-Paul's word of encouragement for us
    1) the people of God often fall (trials & temptations)
    2) but God will raise his people up
    3) never forget that He has raised for us a Savior
    4) everything can be taken from us, except Jesus

Paul Preaches in Antioch in Pisidia-Part 2
(Acts 13:26-41)

Part 1 - *God Raised for Israel a Savior* (vs 16-25)
Part 2 - *God Raised the Savior for Israel* (vs 26-41)

1) This message of salvation has been sent to: (26)
    A) the children of Abraham (the Jews)
    B) God-fearers (Gentiles who believe in the God of Israel)

2) The Jews of Jerusalem Rejected Jesus (27)
    A) did not recognize Him (crucify Him, crucify Him)
    B) expected a military conquering Messiah
    C) triumphal entry 7 cleansing the temple
    D) their rejection of Christ fulfilled prophecy of Isaiah 53

3) They asked Pilate to execute Jesus without cause (28)

4) After His birth, Jesus was buried in a tomb (29)

5) But God raised Him from the dead (30)
    A) men killed & shamed Jesus
    B) but God raised & exalted Him

6) He appeared to His disciples (31)
    A) eyewitness testimony-highest level of evidence
    B) over a period of 40 days (Acts 1:1-3)
    C) 1 Corinthians 15:3-8

7) The good news (32-39)
    A) God's everlasting covenant with David (32-37)
        1) fulfilled what God promised to Israel's fathers (32)

    2) resurrection confirmed Jesus' divine Sonship (33)
      (Psalm 2:7)
    3) Jesus' resurrection to immortality fulfilled Isaiah
      55:3-God's eternal covenant with David (34)
    4) Christ's resurrection fulfilled Psalm 16:10 (35-37)
      a) see also Peter's sermon (Acts 2:27)
      b) David's body decomposed
      c) but Jesus was raised to immortality
  B) <u>Forgiveness through Jesus</u> (38-39)
    1) everyone who believes in Jesus is forgiven
    2) justified (declared righteous) through faith in Jesus
    3) not through the Mosaic Law (Romans 3:20-23)

8) <u>Be careful not to reject Jesus</u> (40-41)
  A) Habakkuk 1:5 (Paul applies it to rejecting Christ)
  B) salvation is in no one else (Acts 4:12)
  C) as many Gentiles are accepting Christ, many Jews are
    rejecting him

9) <u>Conclusion</u>
  A) Israel has constantly fallen, but God continually lifts her
    up (Exodus, Conquest, King David, Messiah)
  B) now God has raised Messiah from the dead
  C) death has been conquered
  D) the Davidic Covenant has been fulfilled
  E) God has provided salvation through Jesus' death &
    resurrection
  F) there is no other way of salvation (Jn 14:6; Ac 4:12)
  G) the Gospel of the resurrection is the good news
  H) this good news must always be the primary emphasis of
    the Church

Jews Reject Paul's Message in Pisidia (Acts 13:42-52)

1) <u>Introduction</u>
 A) Paul preaches the gospel in a synagogue in Antioch of
  Pisidia
 B) God raised for Israel a Savior (vs 16-25)
 C) God raised the Savior for Israel (vs 26-41)

2) <u>Acceptance of the Gospel</u> (vs 42-43)
 A) the Gentiles begged Paul to preach again the next Sabbath
 B) many Jews & proselytes followed Paul & Barnabas
 C) Paul & Barnabas encouraged them to persevere in God's
  grace (perseverance = a sign of true belief; 1 Jn 2:19;
  Jn 15:6; Hb 3:14)

3) <u>Rejection of the Gospel by Jewish Religious Leaders</u> (vs 44-47)
 A) sellout crowd the next Sabbath
 B) the Jewish religious leaders became jealous of Paul &
  Barnabas' popularity (don't envy another's ministry)
 C) envy-Mt 27:18 (Jewish leaders envied Jesus)
 D) they tried to refute Paul's teachings (opposition)
 E) they didn't want the gospel to go to the Gentiles
 F) Gentiles can be saved without converting to Judaism
 G) Paul & Barnabas grew bold (under persecution)
  1) Gospel preached first to the Jews (Rm 1:16)
  2) after Jews reject it, then gospel preached to Gentiles
  3) Paul's strategy (synagogue first, then market place)
 H) Paul quotes Isa 49:6 (light to the Gentiles; Lk 2:32)
  -both Israel & Messiah (this is why Jesus cleansed the
  temple-Court of the Gentiles became a marketplace)
 I) God blessed one nation so that through her all nations
  would be blessed (Gn 12:1-3)
 J) God blesses us to be a blessing to others

4) <u>Gentiles Accept Christ (God-fearers)</u> (vs 48-49)
    A) no longer 2nd class citizens (circumcision not needed)
    B) the Gentiles rejoiced (one in Christ; Gal 3:28)
    C) Jn 10:18 (other sheep) & Rm 11:11-14 (jealous)
    D) appointed to eternal life (predestination-Jn 6:37-40)
    E) believed (free will; my view = conditional predestination)
    F) the Gospel began to spread throughout the region
        (true revival is based on the gospel, not fads)

5) <u>Paul & Barnabas Expelled from the Region</u> (vs 50)
    A) the Jews persuaded influential people to oppose them
        1) devout & prominent women
        2) the chief men of the city
    B) persecution arose; Paul & Barnabas forced to leave

6) <u>Paul & Barnabas went to Iconium</u> (vs 51-52)
    A) Paul & Barnabas shook the dust from their feet
        1) Jews often shook dust off their feet when leaving
          "unclean" Gentile towns
        2) these Jews were not true Jews (Rm 2:28-29)
        3) these Jews were worse than Pagans
        4) Jesus' teaching (Mk 6:11)
    B) Paul & Barnabas went to Iconium
        1) about 90 miles southeast of Antioch Pisidia
        2) the most eastern city of Phrygia
    C) the disciples were filled with joy & the Holy Spirit
        1) no joy = no Holy Spirit (happiness = counterfeit)
        2) no Holy Spirit = no joy (Gal 5:22-23)
        3) true joy despite the persecution

7) <u>Application</u>

    A) get used to rejection & opposition; God's work will always be opposed (Jn 15:16-20; Gal 1:10)

    B) don't envy others when God works through them (1 Cor 12; 3:4-6)

    C) God is in control (despite persecution, those God appointed to salvation believed; Rm 8:28)

    D) God desires all to be saved (2 Pt 3:9; 1 Tm 2:1-6)

    E) in reference to salvation, no distinction between Jew & Gentile (Gal 3:28)

    F) God blesses us to be a blessing to others

    G) the joy of the Lord is our strength (Neh 8:10); we have access to God's joy even when things get tough

Paul & Barnabas Complete
the First Missionary Journey (Acts 14:1-28)

1) Introduction
   A) Acts 13--start of the first missionary journey
   B) sent by the church in Antioch of Syria
   C) Paul & Barnabas preached Gospel on the Island of Cyprus
       & in Antioch of Pisidia (converts & opposition)
   D) Paul & Barnabas flee to Iconium

2) Preaching in Iconium (vs 1-7)
   A) about 90 miles southeast of Antioch of Pisidia
   B) Paul & Barnabas preached in the synagogue
   C) many Jews & Gentiles believed
   D) some Jews rejected the Gospel & convinced Gentiles to
       oppose Paul & Barnabas
   E) Paul & Barnabas spoke boldly (Acts 4:31)
   F) God confirmed their message with signs & wonders
       1) Moses, OT prophets, Jesus, Apostles
       2) Hebrews 2:3-4; 2 Corinthians 12:12; 1 Cor 4:20
   G) the city was divided (Jesus divides--Lk 12:51-53)
   H) Paul & Barnabas called apostles (one sent forth with a
       message & the authority of the sender)
   I) Paul & Barnabas find out about a plot to stone them
   J) they fled to Lycaonian cities of Lystra & Derbe
   K) they continued to preach God's Word

3) Preaching In Lystra (vs 8-20; 18 miles southwest of Iconium)
   A) Paul healed a crippled man from birth
   B) the man had the faith to be healed (Mt 7:6)
       -not "name it & claim it"
   C) the townspeople shouted in the Lycaonian language
   D) they thought Paul & Barnabas were Hermes & Zeus

1) <u>Hermes</u>-the messenger of the gods (Rome-Mercury);
  one of the sons of Zeus
2) <u>Zeus</u>-the father of the gods, but not the creator-god;
  the god of the sky & weather (Rome-Jupiter)
3) Roman poet Ovid told of an ancient legend that
  Hermes & Zeus visited the region disguised as
  humans, destroying homes of those who refused
  to welcome them
E) they wanted to sacrifice to them
F) Paul & Barnabas objected & tore their clothes
 1) we are only human
 2) turn from worthless idols
  -dead, false gods (1 Cor 10:20)
 3) turn to the *living* God of creation
 4) God has been patient with the Gentiles
 5) natural revelation (rain, crops, seasons)
  -Rm 1:18-22; Ps 19:1; Ac 17
G) Jews from Antioch & Iconium convinced the crowd to
  stone Paul & drag him outside the city (2 Tm 3:12)
H) Paul revived & re-entered the city
I) Paul & Barnabas left for Derbe the next day

4) <u>Returning to Antioch of Syria</u> (vs 21-28)
 A) they preached & led many to Christ in Derbe
 B) they returned to Lystra, Iconium, & Antioch of Pisidia
  1) strengthen & encourage the disciples
  2) remain true to the faith
  3) be willing to suffer for Jesus
  4) appointed elders for each church
  5) they prayed with fasting
 C) they went from Pisidia to Pamphylia
  -preached in Perga, went to Attalia
 D) they retraced their steps despite the danger
 E) they sailed back to Antioch of Syria
  1) this ended the first missionary journey

2) they reported to the mother church
3) they remained there for a long time

5) <u>Conclusion--Principles to Apply</u>
    A) be willing to suffer for Jesus
    B) the more people you preach to-the more will accept Jesus
    C) the more people you preach to-the more will reject you
    D) Jesus is the most divisive Person who ever lived
    E) our ministries must be empowered by God
    F) we must reject worship from others
    G) we must turn from worthless idols
        (broken cisterns-Jeremiah 2:13)
    H) strengthen & encourage one another (Hb 10:23-25)
    I) submit to godly leadership (elders)

The Jerusalem Council (Acts 15:1-35)

1) Introduction
   A) Paul & Barnabas completed their 1st missionary journey
   B) they returned to Antioch of Syria & stayed for some time

2) Judaizers cause divisions in Antioch (vs 1-2)
   A) some men came to Antioch from Judea (Jerusalem
      church)
   B) taught the heresy that believers cannot be saved unless
      they are circumcized & obey the Law of Moses
   C) salvation by faith plus works/law
   D) Paul & Baranabas debated them (Eph 2:8-9; Ac 16:31)
   E) it was determined that Paul, Barnabas, & other leaders
      from the Antioch Church needed to meet with the
      apostles & elders of the Jerusalem Church

3) Different views in the early church
   A) Judaizers--also known as legalists; taught salvation by
      faith in Jesus plus obeying the Old Testament Law
      (Paul wrote Galatians to refute this heresy; Gal 1:6-9;
      2:7-9, 16, 21; 3:11, 24-26, 28; 4:10, 11; 5:6; 6:13-15)
   B) Weaker Brothers--taught salvation by faith in Jesus, but
      we mature in Christ by obeying the Old Testament Law;
      they failed to understand our freedom in Christ
      (Romans 14:1-3; 14, 17, 21)
   C) Nazarenes--taught salvation by faith in Jesus; only Jews
      are required to obey the Old Testament Law (James?)
   D) Hellenistic Jewish Christianity--salvation through faith in
      Jesus alone; Jesus fulfilled Old Testament ceremonial
      law (Stephen, Paul, Barnabas)

E) <u>Common Ground</u>--Jewish believers should obey Old
Testament Law for the sole purpose of finding common
ground with non-believing Jews (Paul & possibly
James; 1 Cor 9:19-23)
F) <u>Licentiousness</u>--saved by belief in Jesus; we have a license
to sin (Jm 2:26; Rm 3:31; 6:1, 14; Ju 4)

3) <u>The true View of Salvation</u> (D & E above)
    A) Eph 2:8-10; John 3:16-18; 11:25-26; 14:6
    B) salvation is by God's grace alone through faith alone in
        Jesus alone
    C) however, true saving faith produces good works
    D) good works are not the cause of salvation
    E) good works are the result of salvation

4) <u>Application</u>
    A) theology was important to the early church
        -no church growth councils, no Promise Keepers, etc.
    B) justification by faith alone was not visited by the church
        again until 1517--the Protestant Reformation (Martin
        Luther)
    C) trusting in Jesus plus something else will not save
    D) we must trust in Jesus alone for salvation (Col 2:8-10)
    E) Christ fulfilled the Old Testament Law (Col 2:11-17)
    F) are you trusting in Jesus alone for salvation?

The Jerusalem Council--Part 3 (Acts 15:1-29)

1) Introduction (vs 1-2)
    A) Judaizers from Judea visit Antioch
    B) they taught that Gentiles need to be circumcised to be
        saved (Paul & Barnabas opposed them)
    C) Paul & Barnabas travel to Jerusalem to meet with the
        apostles & elders

2) Paul & Barnabas pass through Phoenicia & Samaria (vs 3)
    A) they described the conversion of the Gentiles
    B) the Phoenicians & Samaritans rejoiced
    C) the best way to oppose falsehoods is to preach the truth

3) Paul & Barnabas in Jerusalem (vs 4)
    A) Paul & Barnabas reported God's work among the Gentiles
        to the leaders of the Jerusalem church
    B) apostles--the authoritative witnesses of Jesus' ministry
    C) elders--also leaders of the Jerusalem church

4) The Pharisees Object (vs 5)
    A) Pharisees--Jewish rabbis who taught in the synagogues
    B) many Pharisees accepted Jesus as the Jewish Messiah
    C) they stated that the Gentiles needed to be circimcized &
        needed to obey the Law of Moses to be saved

5) The Jerusalem Council (vs 6)
    A) the issue was important enough for the apostles & elders
        to hold a church council to settle it
    B) after much dispute, Peter speaks (vs 7-11)
        1) he reminds them how he led Cornelius to Christ
        2) God purified the believing Gentiles' hearts by faith

3) salvation by grace alone through faith alone in Jesus
  alone (see Ephesians 2:8-9)
4) both Jew & Gentile saved the same way
5) even the Jews can't perfectly obey God's Laws
6) Peter's authority was well respected in Jerusalem
C) <u>Paul & Barnabas spoke to the council</u> (vs 12)
  1) Peter paved the way for the apostles to the Gentiles
   to be heard (Galatians 2:9)
  2) Paul & Barnabas related how God had worked
   miracles through them among the Gentiles
  3) 2 Corinthians 12:12; Hebrews 2:3-4
D) <u>James sums up the meeting</u> (vs 13-21)
  1) Peter told what God had done (Acts 10)
  2) Paul & Barnabas told what God was doing
  3) James now relates what God has said
  4) the biblical justification for these experiences
   a) James quotes Amos 9:11-12
   b) ultimately fulfilled in the Millennium
   c) David's tent will be rebuilt when Jesus returns
   d) the Gentiles who are called by My name
  5) James' point--Old Testament speaks of Gentile
   believers (they don't have to become Jews)
  6)God foreknew the conversion of the Gentiles
  7) don't trouble the Gentiles with the burden of the Law
  8) James' ruling--abstain from the following:
   a) things polluted by idols
   b) sexual immorality
   c) strangled animals
   d) blood
  9) Rev 2:14, 20; Col 2:16-17; Rm 14:1-3, 6, 14-20;
   1 Cor 8:4-13; 1 Tim 4:1-4

        10) circumcision & the law are not required for
             salvation (truth)
        11) prohibitions necessary to promote fellowship
             between Jews & Gentiles (unity)
        12) since there are Jews in every city, Gentile believers
             must be sensitive to their concerns (vs 21)

6) <u>The Jerusalem Decree</u> (vs 22-29)
    A) Judas/Barsabas & Silas sent with Paul & Barnabas to
       Antioch to deliver the letter (22) {a Judean & a
       Hellenist}
    B) the Judaizers were not sent by the leaders of the Jerusalem
       church (24)
    C) refers to Paul & Barnabas as "beloved"
    D) defended salvation through faith alone
    E) gave guidelines for fellowship between Jews & Gentiles

7) <u>Paul & Barnabas Return to Antioch of Syria</u> (vs 30-35)
    A) with Judas/Barsabas & Silas (a Judean & a Hellenist)
    B) the letter was read to members of the Antioch Church
    C) the Antioch believers rejoiced
       1) freedom in Christ (no burden of OT Law)
       2) unity in the body of Christ (Jew & Gentile)
       3) Gentiles are not 2nd class citizens in the church
    D) Judas & Silas were prophets (32-34)
       1) they encouraged the Antioch Christians
       2) they returned to Jerusalem? (did Silas stay?)
          a) did others travel with them & Silas stayed?
          b) did Silas return to Jerusalem & later return to
             Antioch? (vs 34 is not in oldest manuscripts)

E) Paul & Barnabas remained in Antioch Preaching & teaching the Word (35)

8) <u>Conclusion</u>

    A) salvation by faith plus works is false gospel

    B) true view--salvation by grace alone through faith alone in Jesus alone (Eph 2:8-9; Jn 3:16-18; 14:6)

    C) early church recognized the importance of both truth & unity (unity within the truth; no unity apart from truth)

    D) we must never allow our freedom in Christ to cause weaker believers to stumble

Paul & Barnabas Quarrel About John Mark:
The God of a Second Chance
Acts 15:36-41

1) Introduction
   A) the Jerusalem Council created great unity in the church
   B) the Jewish & Gentile branches of Christianity were united
   C) the Christians in Antioch rejoiced
      1) not bound to the Law of Moses
      2) not second class Christians

2) Paul & Barnabas decide to visit the churches they planted on their first missionary journey (36)
   A) help disciple the new converts
   B) check on the state of the churches
   C) pass on the decision of the Jerusalem Council to them

3) Paul & Barnabas Disagree about taking John Mark (37-38)
   A) Barnabas wanted John Mark to accompany them (37)
      1) the welfare of the troops came first to Barnabas
      2) he was "the son of encouragement" (Acts 4:36-37)
      3) he was always willing to give someone a second chance (Acts 9:26-27)
      4) he knew John Mark well--John Mark was his cousin (Colossians 4:10)
   B) Paul did not want to take John Mark with them (38)
      1) the mission came first to Paul
      2) John Mark had abandoned them on their first missionary journey (Acts 13:13)
      3) John Mark was young & may have been afraid
      4) John Mark might get in the way

4) <u>The Argument causes Paul & Barnabas to Split</u> (39-41)
    A) the disagreement caused Paul & Barnabas to go separate
       ways
    B) Barnabas took John Mark & ministered at the Island of
       Cyprus (Barnabas' original home--Acts 4:36; churches
       planted there during the first missionary journey)
    C) Paul took Silas & ministered throughout Syria & Cilicia &
       onto other churches planted during the first missionary
       journey (and beyond)
    D) Paul may have selected Silas for several reasons
       1) also a Roman citizen (Acts 16:37-38)
       2) from the mother church (Jerusalem)
       3) a Hellenistic Jew

5) <u>Who Was Right: Paul or Barnabas?</u>
    A) <u>my opinion--ultimately Barnabas was right</u>
       1) John Mark just needed a second chance (as did Paul)
       2) he later wrote the Gospel of Mark
       3) he later became Peter's assistant (1 Peter 5:12)
       4) Paul later acknowledged John Mark's usefulness
         (Col 4:10; Philemon 23-24; 2 Tim 4:11)
       5) Paul was later reunited with Barnabas (1 Cor 9:6)
    B) <u>confirmation? (Paul's next moves--Acts 16:1-3)</u>
       1) Timothy, like John Mark, was a young man from a
         good family (Acts 12:12, 25)
       2) Timothy, like John Mark, was afraid (2 Tm 1:7)
       3) did Timothy remind Paul of John Mark?
       4) did Paul feel guilty about his decision?
       5) our God is the God of a second chance (Eph 4:32)

6) <u>Lessons to Learn</u>
    A) even believers who love Jesus & are doctrinally sound
        may have disagreements about strategy, personalities
    B) believers often have different focuses
        --mission-centered or people-centered
    C) always be willing to forgive & give a second chance
        (remember what Jesus did for us)
    D) God can bring good out of evil
        1) turned one missionary team into two
        2) worked on John Mark's character & Paul's heart
        3) produced a Timothy
        4) modern example--church split = 2 churches

Paul Begins His Second Missionary Journey (Acts 16:1-10)

1)<u>Introduction</u>
    A)Paul & Barnabas return to Antioch of Syria after attending the Jerusalem Council
    B)they decide to start the 2nd missionary journey & visit the churches they had planted
    C)they disagreed about giving John Mark a 2nd chance
    D)Barnabas & John Mark left for the Island of Cyprus
    E) Paul & Silas went through Syria & Cilicia

2)<u>Timothy Joins Paul & Silas</u> (vs 1-3)
    A)Paul & Silas arrived in Derbe & Lystra
    B) a young disciple named Timothy was there
        1)did he remind Paul of John Mark? (2 Tm 1:7)
        2)Timothy had a Jewish Christian mother but a non-believing Gentile father
        3)Timothy had a good reputation among the church
    C)Paul wanted to recruit Timothy for this mission trip
    D)Paul had Timothy circumcised
        1)because his mother was Jewish
        2)so he could have a ministry to Jews (1 Cor 9:19-22)
        3)Paul took a different approach with Titus—a Gentile (Gal 2:1-3; 5:6)
        4)for then it would imply circumcision is necessary for salvation

3)<u>Delivering the Jerusalem Decrees</u> (4-5)
    A)one united church—both Jew & Gentile
    B)salvation by God's grace alone, through faith alone, in Christ alone
    C)circumcision & the ceremonial law are not needed for Salvation
    D)still, Gentile believers must make a clean break from idolatrous practices

E)to fellowship with Jews, Gentile believers should refrain
  from eating meat with blood & food sacrificed to idols
F)the Gentile churches received the decrees well
G)Paul & his team strengthened the churches in their faith
H)the churches grew in numbers daily

4)The Holy Spirit Guides the Missionaries (vs 6-10)
  A)forbidden by the Holy Spirit to preach in Asia
  B)forbidden by God to preach in Bithynia (north)
  C)Paul receives a night vision of a man in Macedonia
   praying for help
  D)the missionary team concludes that God wants them to
   preach in Macedonia, so they go there (Greece—the
   West)
  E)"we"—Luke the author now joins the missionary team
  F)God sends & leads missionaries (Rm 10:14-15)
  G)if someone seeks the Lord from a distant land, God will
   send missionaries to him
    1)creation/conscience (Rm 1:18-22; 2:14-15; Ps 19:1)
    2)Jn 16:7-11; Jm 4:8
    3)Ps 145:18-19; Jer 29:13

5)Conclusions—Lessons We Can Learn
  A)disciple younger Christians (John Mark, Timothy, Titus)
   --God's work continues after you're gone
  B)follow-up on new converts—disciple them if possible
  C)plant churches for new converts
  D)don't add conditions to salvation
  E)become all things to all men—find common ground
  F)promote the unity of the church
  G)don't be a stumbling block to others (eating food)
  H)bring others into the fold (evangelize & disciple)
  I)follow the guidance of the Holy Spirit

A Tale of 2 Ladies (Acts 16:11-24)

1)Introduction
    A)Paul's 2nd missionary journey (with Silas, Timothy, Luke)
    B)called to Macedonia to preach
2)Lydia (vs 11-15)
    A)missionary team sailed from Troas to Samothrace &
        Neapolis, then traveled to Philippi (vs 11-12)
    B)Philippi—foremost city of that part of Macedonia
        1)named after the father of Alexander the Great
        2)a Roman colony loyal to the Empire
        3)area settled by Roman army veterans who were given
            the rights of citizenship
        4)a major commercial center; a very influential city
    C)Paul's strategy—preach in synagogues first in every city
    D)apparently no synagogue in Philippi (13)
        1)according to Jewish custom, a synagogue
          congregation consisted of at least 10 households
        2)at least 10 male heads of households were needed
        3)if no synagogue could be formed, Jews & God-
          fearing Gentiles would meet for prayer at a river side
        4)lack of godly male leadership
    E)Lydia accepts Christ (14-15)
        1)a seller of purple dye, from Thyatira originally
        2)she worshiped God (a true God-seeker)
        3)she accepted Christ/God opened her heart—Jn 12:32
        4)she & her household were baptized
        5)she was gifted in hospitality—missionary team stayed
          at her house ("faithful to the Lord")
        6)the importance of hospitality for early Christianity
          (2 Jn 10-11; 3 Jn 5-10; Mt 25:34-40; Mk 6:7-11)
3)The Demon-Possessed Slave Girl (vs 16-24)
    A)possessed with a spirit of divination
        1)literally—"a spirit of Puthonos," Python (16)
          A)mythical serpent killed by Apollo

        B)the serpent's ability to predict the future was
           given to Apollo who sometimes took the
           form of a serpent

    2)divination & fortune-telling (demonic power)
        A)forbidden in the Bible (Deut 18:9-12; Isa 8:19)
        B) popular in America today (psychic hotline)

    3)through fortune-telling she brought great wealth to
        her masters (once again a growth industry)

    4)she followed the missionary team many days (17)
        A)crying out, "these men are slaves (douloi) of
          the Most High God, who proclaim to us a way
          of salvation (hodon soterias)
        B)Jesus never allowed demons to preach His
          Word (Mk 1:23-26; credibility & deception)

    5)Paul got annoyed cast the demon out of her (18)
        A)in the name of Jesus (will, authority)
        B)the demon left immediately (Ex 7:10-12)

    6)her masters were angry—their business was hurt (19)

    7)they seized Paul & Silas & took them to the officials

    8)Paul & Silas--beaten with rods & imprisoned (20-24)
        A)charge—Jews teaching customs not lawful for
          Romans (paganism protected by law;
           Christianity is illegal; USA today—Isa 5:20)
        B)beaten with rods (2 Cor 11:23-25)
        C)thrown into the inner prison with their feet
          secured in the stocks

4)<u>Conclusion—Application for Americans Today</u>
    A)Lydia--the traditional, God-fearing, hospitable woman
        (Prov 31:30)
    B)the demon-possessed slave girl (new age pagan)
    C)the politically-correct, neo-pagan wealthy & masses
    D)Christians willing to suffer for Jesus (Jn 15:18-20; 16:33)

The Philippian Jailer
(Acts 16:25-40)

1)Introduction--Paul & Silas were arrested for casting a demon out
    of a fortune-telling slave girl in Philippi

2)Paul & Silas' response to suffering & persecution (vs 25)
    A)praying & singing hymns at midnight
        1)during trials we need to follow Paul's example
        2)1 Thes 5:16-18; Rm 5:3-5; Mt 5:10-12; Jm 1:2-4;
            1 Pt 4:12-17)
    B)the prisoners were listening to them
        1)epekroonto = to listen attentively
        2)prison ministries can be very effective—prisoners are
            usually looking for answers (reminded of guilt)
        3)others are watching us & listening to what we say
        4)we are Christ's representatives (Ac 1:8; 2 Cor 5:20)

3)the earthquake (vs 26)
    A)sometimes God chooses to deliver us from our sufferings
    B)sometimes He does not (2 Tm 4:6-7; 18)
    C)prisoners freed, but they did not flee (revival?)

4)the jailer prepares to kill himself (vs 27)
    A)he thought the prisoners would escape
    B)he was ready to commit suicide to protect his family's
        honor—it would appear that he died valiantly

5)Paul convinces the jailer to refrain from suicide (vs 28)
    A)he tells the jailer that none had escaped
    B)did the prisoners become Christians?
    C)salvation of the jailer was more important than physical
        Freedom for Paul & Silas

6)the jailer asked Paul & Silas what he must do to be saved (vs 30)
    A)was he listening to Paul & Silas praising God before he
    fell asleep? Was he aware of the ministry of Paul & Silas, or
    the slave girl's declaration about them?

7)Paul's response (vs 31)
    A)believe on the Lord Jesus Christ & you will be saved
    B)you & your household (if they believe as well)
        --Paul knew the jailer cared about his family
    C)believe = pisteuo (trust in, rely upon)
    D)the Lord (kurios = Yahweh; Jesus is God)
    E)Jesus (Jesus really became a man)
    F)Christ (christos = the Jewish Messiah)
    G)the only condition for salvation, according to Paul, was
        that a person believe in the true Jesus of the Bible
        alone for salvation (Jn 3:16-18; 14:6)
    H)Paul was opposed to adding additional requirements for
        salvation (Acts 15; Gal; Eph 2:8-10)

8)the jailer & his family accept Christ & are baptized (vs 32-34)
    A)Paul explained more thoroughly the Gospel message (32)
        1)to the entire family of the jailer
        2)are you to prepared to share the Gospel?
    B)the jailer & his family believe & are baptized (33)
        --the jailer then washes their wounds (1 Jn 4:20-21)
    C)the new believers rejoiced & fed Paul & Silas (34)

9)Paul & Silas are released (35-40)
    A)the next morning they were to be released (35-36)
    B)Paul informs them that he & Silas are Roman citizens (37)
        1)they had been beaten & imprisoned without a fair
            trial (their rights had been violated)

2)Paul & Silas would not leave unless the authorities escorted them out of the prison

3)Paul only exercised his rights to further the cause of the gospel & to protect the brethren (Mt 5:38-48; Rm 12:17-21)

C)the magistrates were afraid (38-39)
  1)they didn't want to get in trouble
  2)they apologized & escorted them out
  3)they asked Paul & Silas to depart the city
  4)they didn't want further trouble
D)Paul & Silas went to Lydia's house (40)
  1)they encouraged the brethren there
  2)then they departed for Thessalonica

10)Conclusion
  A)we must be willing to suffer for Christ (2 Tm 3:12)
  B)we must experience the joy of the Lord despite our circumstances (Rm 8:28; Neh 8:10; Ps 30:5)
  C)remember that people are watching you & listening to what you say (especially when times are bad)
  D)remember you represent Jesus all the time
  E)don't add to the Gospel—salvation is by God's grace alone through faith alone in Jesus alone
  F)like the jailer, we must care for our brothers & sisters
  G)don't be overly concerned about your rights (unless it furthers the cause of the Gospel or aids others)

Paul Preaches in Thessalonica (Acts 17:1-9)

1)Introduction
    A)Paul & Silas set free from Philippian jail
    B)they leave Philipi

2)Paul in Thessalonica (1-9)
    A)62 miles west of Philippi
    B)Paul's custom—preach first in synagogues, then market
        places after Jews reject Gospel
    C)Paul preached in Thessalonica synagogue (vs 1-3)
        1)for 3 Sabbaths he reasoned with the Jews
        2)from the Scriptures (Old Testament)
        3)proving Messiah had to suffer, die, & rise
        4)proving Jesus is the Messiah (conqueror?)
        5)Genesis 3:15; Zechariah 12:10; Daniel 9:26;
            Isaiah 52:13-53:12; Psalm 22:1-18; 16:10
    D)the results of Paul's preaching (vs 4-6)
        1)some of the Jews were converted
        2)many Gentiles/God-fearers accepted Christ
            (1 Thessalonians 1:9)
        3)leading women of the city (wealthy, influential)
        4)Jews who weren't persuaded became jealous
        5)they incited a riot by recruiting the "evil men of the
            marketplace" (agoraion = market-loafers; thugs;
            they hung out, looked for trouble, & would do
            anything for pay)
        6)the mob dragged Jason & others out of his house to
            the rulers of the city (Paul & Silas had escaped)
        7)Jason—a convert (Paul & Silas stayed at his house)
        8)politarchas-found nowhere else in Greek literature;
            once considered an error by Luke; now 17
            inscriptions have been found with this word for
            city leaders (5 from Thessalonica)

E)the charges (vs 6-7)

    1)they turned the world upside down (causing disturbances; the Gospel was impacting the ancient world)

    2)they proclaim Jesus as King, not Caesar (a rival to the throne—treason)

        a)Paul preached much about the end times there

        b)2 Thessalonians 2:5 (1 Thes 4, 5; 2 Thes 1, 2, 3)

        c)Jesus will bring God's Kingdom to earth (Ps 2)

        d)He will defeat all earthly kings (Ps 110:1)

F)Jason released (vs 8-9)

    1)Jason had to pay a bond he would forfeit if there were any further disturbances

    2)they released Jason & his colleagues

    3)the leaders were actually after Paul & Silas who had escaped

    4)Paul & Silas will go to Berea & receive a much warmer welcome

3)Conclusion

A)be willing to suffer rejection for sharing the Gospel

B)the Bible is our only offensive weapon for spiritual warfare—are you an expert with your weapon? (Eph 6:17)

    1)can you lead a person to Christ from the Scriptures?

    2)can you prove Jesus is Savior, Messiah, or God from the Bible?

    3)can you refute heresies with the Bible?

C)are we turning our community upside down?

D)do we proclaim Jesus as our King?

E)are we offending people enough? (1 Cor 1:23; Jn 15:18)

F)it's not our goal to offend, but it comes with the turf

The Noble-Minded Bereans (Acts 17:10-15)

1)Introduction
    A)Paul preached in the synagogue in Thessalonica
    B)he started a church there, but was run out of town
    C)now he travels 40 miles southwest to Berea

2)Paul & Silas Preach in Berea (vs 10-12)
    A)Paul & Silas sent away by night to Berea to escape
        persecution—they preached in the Berean synagogue
    B)the Bereans were more open to the Gospel than the
      Thessalonians were (fair, noble, open-minded)
        1)they received Paul's message eagerly
        2)they diligently study the scriptures each day
        3)anakrino = to examine, investigate, carefully research
        4)they tested Paul's teachings with the Word of God
        5)2 Tm 2:15; 3:16-17; 1 Thes 5:21
    C)the result—many Bereans believed
        --many Jews, Greeks, & prominent men & women (i.e.,
        leading families of the city)

3)Jews From Thessalonica Went to Berea (vs 13-15)
    A)they learned that Paul was preaching in Berea
    B)they went to Berea to stir up the crowds
    C)the brethren immediately sent Paul to the Mediterranean
        Sea, but Silas & Timothy remained in Berea
    D)Paul was sent to Athens; he sent for Silas & Timothy

4)Conclusion—Do we diligently study God's Word everyday to
    learn God's truth? (Ps 1;1-3; Eph 6:17)

Paul Preaches on Mars Hill
(Acts 17:16-21) Parts One & Two

1)Introduction
      A)Paul flees Berea & arrives in Athens
      B)as Paul waited for Timothy & Silas, he debated in the
           synagogue & marketplace (the Agora; vs 16-21)
      C)eventually Paul was invited to speak on Mars Hill
           (Areopagus; vs 22-31)
      D)the response of the Athenians will be mixed (vs 32-34)
      E)an example of how Paul preached to educated Pagans

2)Paul's Spirit was Provoked Within Him (vs 16)
      A)when he saw the city was filled with idols
      B)Ex 20:1-6; 1 Cor 10:20; Rm 1:18-25
      C)great philosophers had taught at Athens throughout the
           centuries: Socrates, Plato, Aristotle, Epicurus, & Zeno
      D)the best of Greek philosophy couldn't stifle idolatry in the
           West; only Christianity could do this
      E)Pliny—1st century Athens had over 30,000 public idols
      F)Petronius—easier to find a god in Athens than a man

3)This Caused Paul to Preach Jesus Daily (vs 17)
      A)he reasoned in the synagogue from OT Hebrew scriptures
           --with Jews & Gentiles (God-fearers)
      B)he reasoned with Greeks in the marketplace (the Agora)

4)Epicurean & Stoic Philosophers Confront Paul (vs 18)
      A)Epicurean Philosophy
           1)Epicurus (340-272 BC)
           2)practical atheism/deism (the gods are not concerned
                 with the affairs of man)
           3)no life after death; pleasure is the goal of life

B)<u>Stoic Philosophy</u>
    1)Zeno of Citium (340-265 BC) {not the famous Zeno}
    2)pantheistic/world-soul/globally focused
    3)focused on reason & man's self-sufficiency
    4)universe has a rational structure (logos; nous)
    5)fate controls the future; everything happens with
        necessity (no human free will)
    6)attitude of indifference; lack of passion
C)<u>they called Paul a "babbler"</u> (spermologos = a seed picker)
    --a pseudo-philosopher who steals ideas from real
        thinkers; collection of sound bites, no deep thought
D)<u>they accused Paul of proclaiming strange or foreign gods</u>
    1)gods = daimonion (Greek gods were demons)
    2)Jesus & Resurrection (they misunderstood Paul)
    3)Resurrection (anastasis = a female deity)
    4)Roman Law prohibited teaching new religions
E)<u>they brought Paul to Areopagus</u> (vs 19-20)
    1)Mars Hill = Hill of Ares (the Greek God of war)
    2)to hear his views, not to legally try him
    3)a council that heard & judged philosophical ideas
F)<u>the Athenians' favorite hobby</u> (vs 21)
    1)the exchange of new ideas
    2)they spent their day discussing philosophy
    3)philosophy = love of wisdom

5)<u>Conclusion</u>
    A)do we use our "down time" to share Jesus with others?
    B)are our spirits greatly provoked by paganism & idolatry?
    C)do we study the ideas of non-Christian thinkers so we can
        dialogue with new agers, atheists, & religious liberals?
    D)1 Cor 1:18-24, 30-31; 1 Cor 2:1-8; Col 2:8-10

Paul Preaches on Mars Hill (Part Three)
(Acts 17:22-34)

1)Introduction
    A)Paul is asked to speak at the Aereopagus (Mars Hill)
    B)before Stoic & Epicurean philosophers
    C)they thought he proclaimed 2 deities--Jesus & Resurrection
2)Paul's Sermon on Mars Hill (vs 22-31)
    A)Paul finds common ground (vs 22)
        1)"very religious" (he saw their many idols)
        2)1 Corinthians 9:19-22
        3)common ground essential to be persuasive
    B)the Unknown God (vs 23)
        1)just in case they missed one, the Greeks built altars to
            the unknown god
        2)Paul uses this as an opportunity to preach the Gospel
        3)he tells them he knows the one God they don't know
        4)this God happens to be the only true God
    C)Paul preaches about the unknown God (vs 24-31)
        1)He is the Creator of everything (24)
          --not demiurgos (matter not eternal or evil)
        2)He is the Lord of everything
          a)He is sovereign (in control; He rules universe)
          b)not a local deity
        3)He doesn't dwell in man-made temples (transcendent)
    D)He is all-sufficient (25)
        1)He doesn't need man's help
        2)He doesn't need anything (independent/transcendent)
        3)we are totally dependent on Him for life, breath, and
            all things (immanent)
    E)He created all people from one man (26)
        1)false view—different gods created different races
        2)false dichotomy—Greeks & Barbarians
        3)the human race is one race

       4)one family through creation; not redemption

       5)God is sovereign—He predetermined our times &
          places (so that we would seek Him)

F)God is not far from any man (27)

       1)He predetermined when & where we would live so
          that we would seek Him

       2)Jer 29:13; Jn 12:32; Jm 4:8

       3)God is near to all who call on Him in truth

       4)Ps 145:18-19 (immanence)

G)Paul quotes from ancient Greek poets (28)

       1)finding more common ground

       2)persuasion often involves taking a person from their
          premises to your conclusion

       3) "in Him we live and move and have our being"

          a)attributed to Epimenides the Cretan (600BC)

          b)our total dependence on God; not pantheism

          c)not Zeus or a pantheistic god, but the true
             Creator God

       4) "we are His offspring"

          a)attributed to Aratus of Cilicia (310BC)

          b)He made us; we didn't make Him

          c)not Zeus or a pantheistic god, but the true
             Creator God

H)God is not a man-made idol (29)

       --both Stoics & Epicureans would agree

I)God is patient (30)

       1)He didn't destroy the Greeks for their idolatry

       2)He overlooked their ignorance

       3)now commands all men everywhere to repent

       4)to turn from idols to the true God (1 Thes 1:9)

J)the Judgment Day has been set by God (31)

       1)God will judge the world in righteousness

       2)He has appointed the Man named Jesus to be judge

        3)He proved Jesus is the judge by raising Him from the dead (Greeks denied physical resurrection)

        4)Greeks believed physical realm was evil or less than real—no place for a resurrection, only immortality of the soul (maybe reincarnation, but not resurrection)

3)The Mixed Response to Paul's Sermon (vs 32-34)

    A)some mocked—resurrection was anti-intellectual from their perspective

    B)some wanted to hear more

    C)some believed

        1)Dionysius (a member of the Mars Hill council)

          --Eusebius reported that he became the first bishop of Athens

        2)a woman named Damaris

        3)and others

    D)no mention of a church being planted there

    E)the first fruits of Achaia lived in Corinth, not Athens (1 Cor 16:15)

    F)Paul left & departed for Corinth (18:1)

4)Conclusion—Follow Paul's Example

    A)find common ground—go out of your way to compliment

    B)study the views of non-Christian thinkers

    C)know your audience & find a way to present the gospel to Them, but never compromise the gospel

    D)we must preach the cross, resurrection, & judgment even if it is not popular

    E)we must preach God's truth & leave the results to God

    F)are we able to preach to atheists (Epicureans) & pantheists (Stoics), even when its not politically correct?

Paul Ministers in Corinth (Acts 18:1-23)

1)<u>Introduction</u>—after preaching on Mars Hill in Athens, Paul
    travels to another Greek city—Corinth

2)<u>Paul leaves Athens & goes to Corinth</u> (vs 1)
    A)Corinth was the political capital of Achaia (Greece)
    B)also, a prosperous commercial center
    C)great potential for evangelism & church planting
    D)a center of Aphrodite worship (a goddess of fertility)
        1)sexual immorality was widespread in Corinth
        2)a 5th century BC Roman saying denoting sexual
            promiscuity—"to act like a Corinthian"
    E)Corinth also had an important temple devoted to the
        worship of the Greek god Apollo (god of art, science,
        & self-control)

3)<u>Paul Meets Aquila & Priscilla</u> (vs 2-3)
    A)Aquila was a Jew originally from Pontus (a province in
        northern Asia Minor)
    B)he & his wife Priscilla had recently come from Rome
    C)Emperor Claudius ordered certain Jews to leave Rome due
        to riots instigated by "Chrestus" {49AD} (Suetonius)
    D)most likely rioting of the Jews due to the preaching of the
        gospel in Rome
    E)Aquila & Priscilla owned a tentmaker business
    F)they hired Paul (Paul was often bi-vocational)
    G)1 Cor 9:3-18; Mt 10:5-10; Lk 10:7; 1 Tm 5:17-18
    H)Aquila & Priscilla were not converts of Paul
        1)Feast of Pentecost? (Acts 2:9-10)
        2)may have helped found the church of Rome
    I)they were a great missionary team (helper—Genesis 2)

4)Paul debated in the Synagogues every Sabbath (vs 4)
      A)argued that Jesus is the Jewish Messiah & the Savior
      B)his audience = Jews & Gentile God-fearers

5)Silas & Timothy arrived in Corinth (vs 5)
      A)they came from Macedonia (Berea)
      B)Paul left them in Berea—Acts 16:13-15
      C)Paul had ministered alone in Athens (little fruit)
      D)in Corinth—joined by Aquila, Priscilla, Silas, & Timothy
      E)unlike Athens, a church will be established in Corinth
      F)in the synagogues, Paul argued that Jesus is the Messiah

6)the Corinthian Jews reject the Gospel (vs 6)
      A)we are not responsible for our hearers' rejection of the
            Gospel if we speak the truth in love (Eph 4:15)
      B)Paul's strategy in each city—preach first to the Jews; when
            they reject the Gospel, preach to the Gentiles

7)Paul preaches in the house of Justice (vs 7)
      A)Titius Justice—a Gentile God-fearer
      B)may have also been called Gaius (1 Cor 1:14; Rm 16:23)
      C)his house was next to the synagogue

8)Crispus—ruler of the Synagogue accepts Christ (vs 8)
      A)all his household also believed (1 Cor 1:14)
      B)many Corinthians heard, believed, & were baptized
      C)the Corinthian church is building (early 50's AD)

9)Jesus appears to Paul in a vision (vs 9-10)
      A)don't be afraid; boldly speak
      B)Paul won't be harmed in Corinth
      C)words of comfort

10)Paul ministered a year and a half in Corinth (vs 11)
    --teaching & discipling & building the church

11)Paul arrested & brought before the authorities (vs 12-17)
    A)Gallio—proconsul of Achaia (Greece) 51-52AD
    B)Gallio—brother of the famous Roman Stoic philosopher
        Seneca (the Stoics were pantheists)
    C)the Jewish leaders arrested Paul & brought him to the
        Roman official, but Gallio refused to try Paul
    D)Paul didn't even have to defend himself
    E)Gallio considered it to be a debate within the Jewish faith;
        Judaism was protected by Roman Law (exemption)
    F)the Greeks beat Sosthenes—the new Synagogue ruler; not
        a believer; not the result the Jewish leaders expected
    G)Gallio decided to ignore the brutality against Sosthenes

12)Paul, Aquila, & Priscilla set sail for Antioch of Syria (vs 18-23)
    A)Antioch of Syria—Paul's home church
    B)they temporarily stopped at Ephesus
    C)he took a Nazarite vow (Num 6—head shaved, no alcohol)
        1)vows often taken to thank God (protection?)
        2)enroute to Jerusalem to celebrate a Jewish Feast
        3)in the temple, the new grown hair was to be shaved &
            burned with the offering
        4)symbolized offering oneself to God
    D)the missionary team left Ephesus en route to Antioch &
        Jerusalem, promising to return to Ephesus
    E)1 Corinthians written while in Ephesus during that future
        visit there—after the Jewish Feast (1 Cor 16:19)
    F)they landed at Caesarea, went up to Jerusalem for the Feast
    G)then went to the home church at Antioch
    H)this completed his 2nd missionary journey

I)Paul spent some time in Antioch

J)then he began his third missionary journey, going to the
      regions of Galatia & Phrygia, strengthening the
      believers there

13)<u>Conclusion</u>

A)God keeps His promises—Paul was not harmed at Corinth

B)Romans 8:28—God works all things for good—Aquila &
      Priscilla kicked out of Rome, meet Paul, & join his
      missionary team (Rome failed to rid its empire of
      Christianity; instead they helped it spread)

C)we're responsible for sharing the Gospel; we're not
      responsible for the response of our hearers

D)we must preach the Word to both Jew & Gentile
      --Matthew 28:19-20; 10:32-33

E)we must strengthen & disciple our converts; thus
      equipping them for service (Eph 4:11-12)

Apollos:Defender of the Faith (Acts 18:24-28)

1)Introduction
    --while Paul visited Jerusalem & the Antioch Church, a man
        named Apollos began to preach in the Ephesian synagogues

2)Apollos (vs 24-26)
    A)a Jew (by nationality & faith)
    B)born in Alexandria, Egypt
        1)2nd largest city in the Roman Empire
        2)a northern seaport of Egypt
        3)founded by Alexander the Great
        4)one-fourth of the population was Jewish
        5)Greeks, Romans, Egyptians there as well
        6)Septuagint translated there about 150BC
        7)had the ancient world's largest library & a university
        8)had replaced Athens as the world's intellectual capital
        9)Philo—famous Jewish philosopher may have been
            alive in Alexandria at that time (Platonic ideas are
            the eternal thoughts of God; logos doctrine)
        10)Clement of Alexandria, Origen, Arius, Athanasius,
            & author of the Epistle of Barnabas
    C)an eloquent man (logios—learned, skilled in literature &
        the art of persuasion)
    D)mighty in the Scriptures (dunatos—from dunamis;
        powerful; well-versed)
    E)Apollos came to Ephesus
        1)the capital of Roman province of Asia (part of
            modern Turkey)
        2)an important commercial center
        3)had a famous temple of the fertility goddess Diana—
            also called Artemis (one of the 7 wonders of
            ancient world)

F)trained in the way of the Lord
    1)John the Baptist (visits to Judea; Mt 3:11-12; Jn 1:29;
        Mt 11:2-6)
    2)Alexandrian synagogues
    3)Pentecost—Egyptians present—Acts 2
    4)probably knew Jesus is Messiah, Savior, suffered,
        died, rose
    5)he spoke & taught accurately the things of the Lord
G)fervent in spirit (zeon—to be hot, to boil; passionate)
H)though he knew only the baptism of John (Mt 3:11-12)
    1)John's baptism—for repentance of sin & preparation
        for coming of Messiah
    2)he never heard of Jesus' baptism (Mt 28:19-20)
        a)identify with Jesus in His baptism &
            resurrection
        b)acknowledge that Jesus baptizes with the Holy
            Spirit—we're new creations (2 Cor 5:17)
    3)baptized into Body of Christ; baptized with Holy
        Spirit (1 Cor 12:13)
I)he spoke boldly in the synagogue
    --parresiazesthai—to speak fearlessly, with courage &
    confidence

3)Aquila & Priscilla help Apollos (vs 26)
    A)they heard him preach in the synagogue
    B)they took him aside (made sure not to embarrass him)
    C)they spoke the truth in love (Eph 4:15)
    D)gently explained the way of God to him more accurately
        (I.e., fully?)

4)Apollos travels to Achaia (vs 27)
    A)he planned to go to Corinth/Greece (Acts 19:1)

B)believers (Aquila & Priscilla?) wrote to disciples there to
   receive him (2 Jn 9-11; 3 Jn 5-12)
C)when he arrived, he greatly helped the believers there
   --2 possible meanings:
     1)they believed through grace (without God's grace, we
       would not believe-divine revelation & persuasion)
     2)or, by Apollos' spirtual gift (teaching) he greatly
       helped the believers in Achaia

5)Apollos preaches in Achaia (vs 28)
   A)he vigorously refuted the Jews publicly
     1)euthonos—strenuously & convincingly
     2)he defeated the Jewish rabbis in public debate
   B)showing from the Scripture (the Old Testament)
   C)that Jesus is the Christ (Messiah—Isa 53; Ps 22; etc.)

6)Conclusion
   A)Apollos' impact in Corinth (vs 19:1)
   B)1 Cor 1:12-13 (they focused on messenger, not message)
   C)1 Cor 3:4-8; 16:12 (no competition between believers)
     --same team—we serve Jesus (unity)
   D)we must defend the faith (1 Pt 3:15; Col 4:5-6; Titus 1:9)
   E)good teachers = good learners/always want to learn more
   F)teach others gently—speak the truth in love—Aquila &
     Priscilla took Apollos aside & advised him privately
   G)Luther believed Apollos wrote the Book of Hebrews
     1)author was a Jew who never met Jesus
     2)personally knew Timothy
     3)author familiar with Pauline theology
     4)used Alexandrian philosophy, terminology, &
       argumentation
     5)Hebrews written before 70AD (temple priests)

Paul in Ephesus: Disciples, Debates, & Demons (Acts 19:1-20)

1)Introduction (Acts 18:19-21)
    --Paul returns to Ephesus as he had promised
2)Twelve Ephesian disciples receive the Holy Spirit (vs 1-7)
    A)while Apollos was at Corinth
    B)Paul came to Ephesus
    C)he found twelve disciples
        1)of Jesus or of John the Baptist?
        2)Paul sensed their spiritual knowledge was deficient
        3)he asked them if they received the Holy Spirit when
            they believed-they replied that they never heard of
            the Holy Spirit
        4)they had yet to receive Christian baptism—they were
            only baptized into John's baptism for repentance
            (Mt 3:11-12)
        5)they may have believed Jesus was the Messiah but
            knew little about Him (Mt 11:2-6)
        6)they then received Christian baptism
        7)Paul, laid hands on them, baptizing them with the
            Holy Spirit (apostolic authority—2 Cor 12:12)
        8)they received the Holy Spirit
        9)evidenced by speaking in tongues & prophesying
        10)transitional stage—Old Testament saints becoming
            New Testament saints; Gospel first preached; start
            of the church
        11)now, all believers are baptized with the Holy Spirit,
            but not all speak in tongues (1 Cor 12:13, 30)
3)Paul preaches for 3 months in the Ephesian synagogue (8)
    A)spoke boldly (courageous proclamation)
    B)reasoning & persuading (discussion & debate)
    C)concerning the Kingdom of God (salvation of man & the
        future deliverance of the earth & Israel by Messiah)
    D)Paul's strategy—preach Gospel to Jews first; when they
        reject the message, go to the Gentiles

4)Paul lectures for 2 years in the School of Tyrannus (9-10)
    A)when the Jews rejected Paul's message in the synagogue,
        Paul went to the Gentiles
    B)the School of Tyrannus—a philosophy lecture hall
    C)Paul taught there for 2 years—Ephesus became a major
        center for the Gentile mission
    D)his disciples began to preach throughout Asia (modern
        Turkey)
    E)Asia was saturated with the Gospel message
    F)the 7 churches of the Book of Revelation may have been
        planted at this time
5)God displays His power in Ephesus (11-20)
    A)Ephesus was a leading center of sorcery, the magic arts,
        the occult, & idolatry
    B)unusual miracles through Paul (11-12)
        1)dunameis = works of power (dynamite)
        2)handkerchiefs & aprons of Paul used to heal people &
            cast out demons (power encounter—Eph 6:10-12)
        3)Paul probably used these cloths while tentmaking
    C)the 7 sons of Sceva (13-17)
        1)traveling Jewish exorcists (some dabbled with the
            Occult & magic—they used incantations)
        2)some started using Jesus' name to cast out demons,
            but they were not believers
        3)one example—the 7 sons of Sceva
        4)Sceva—a Jewish chief priest (he may have been a
            member of the high priest's family)
        5)the demon knew Jesus (ginosko—personal
            knowledge) & was familiar with Paul
            (epistamai—head knowledge)
        6)the demon overpowered them
        7)they fled naked & wounded

        8)fear spread throughout Ephesus among Jews &
           Gentiles; Jesus' name was magnified

        9)the demons knew & feared Jesus

        10)using Jesus' name without believing in Him could
           be detrimental to one's health

    D)repentance & revival in Ephesus (18-20)

        1)no revival without repentance

        2)we cannot have revival in America until we start
           burning our idols

        3)fear of the Lord (Prov 1:7)

        4)new believers shared their testimonies & confessed
           their sins

        5)those who practiced the magic arts burned their books

        6)a large bonfire; books of magic spells & incantations

        7)worth 50,000 pieces of silver (200 yrs wages)

        8)true repentance makes a clean break with the past

        9)God's Word spread throughout the region

6)Conclusion

    A)never assume church members already know the Gospel
      message

    B)ask for the Holy Spirit to empower you (Lk 11:9-13)

    C)share & defend the gospel with both Jew & Gentile

    D)demons fear Jesus, not magic formulas

    E)God is more powerful than the demonic realm
      (Ex 7:10-12)

    F)burn the sins of your past—deny self & follow Jesus;
      don't look back (Mk 8:34; Lk 9:62)

    G)true repentance always precedes true revival

    H)no repentance, no revival

The Riot in Ephesus (Acts 19:21-41)

1)Introduction
- A)Paul is on his 3rd missionary journey
- B)he preached at Ephesus for about 2 ½ years, building the church there, teaching at the School of Tyrannus
- C)many converts publicly burned their occultic books

2)Paul plans to visit Rome (vs 21-22)
- A)after 2 ½ years in Ephesus, it was time for Paul to move on
- B)Paul desired to go to Rome on way to Spain-Rm 15:20-26
- C)but, first he would visit churches in Macedonia & Achaia (regions of ancient Greece), & then go to Jerusalem
- D)trip to Jerusalem to deliver donations (1 Cor 16:1-4; Rm 15:20-26)
- E)Paul sent Timothy & Erastus ahead of him to Macedonia & Achaia
- F)Paul made his plans in the Spirit-Eph 6:18; Gal 5:16-18, 25

3)The Riot in Ephesus (vs 23-41)
- A)great commotion about the Way (23)
  - --the gospel causes controversy (Mt 10:34-36)
- B)Demetrius the silversmith (24-27)
  - 1)made silver shrines of the false goddess Diana
  - 2)Diana = Artemis
  - 3)making idols of Diana was a major Ephesian industry
  - 4)Demetrius called together other idol-makers
    - a)he charged Paul with destroying worship of Diana throughout the province of Asia
    - b)he appealed to their love of money (Paul was bad for their business; 1 Tm 6:10; Mt 6:24)
    - c)Paul refuted the worshiping of manmade idols

C)the false goddess Diana/Artemis
    1)Latin = Diana; Greek = Artemis
    2)the idols were images of a multi-breasted goddess
    3)blended with the Semitic moon goddess Ashtoreth
    4)the Ephesians believed Diana was the great nursing
        mother of the gods, men, animals, & plants
    5)her temple in Ephesus was one of the 7 wonders of
        the ancient world (127 pillars—each 60 feet high)
    6)the temple's foundations were found in 1869; the
        altar was found in 1965
D)the riot begins (vs 28-34)
    1)the crowd cried "Great is Diana of the Ephesians"
    2)they rushed in the theater & seized Gaius &
        Aristarchus—two of Paul's colleagues (the theater
        could seat 25,000 people)
    3)Paul wanted to address the crowd, but disciples
        (including government officials of Asia) would
        not allow him to go to the theater
    4)the crowd was confused—some didn't even know
        why they were there
    5)the Jews put forth Alexander to speak for them—
        don't blame the Jews for Paul's teachings
    6)the crowd would not let him speak & chanted for
        about 2 hours
E)the city clerk brings order (35-41)
    1)he quieted the crowd & spoke
    2)the image of Diana which fell down from Zeus
        (heaven); possibly a meteorite
    3)no one can deny this happened; this was no manmade
        idol
    4)Christians did not rob their temple, nor did they speak
        against Diana

5)if Demetrius really has a case, let him bring it before the government officials

6)if things are not handled orderly, Rome may inflict the city with severe penalties

7)he then dismissed the assembly

8)Pagans & Jews opposed the early spread of Christianity, but, at this time, the Roman government took a fairly tolerant view of the new faith (things would soon change)

4)<u>Application</u>

A)we, like Paul, need to be led by the Holy Spirit (prayer, devotional Bible study, fellowship, etc.)

B)we need the Holy Spirit to guide us in our decisions

C)preaching the Gospel will cause controversy

D)we must be willing to suffer for Christ

E)preaching the Gospel might even destroy people's livelihoods (bars, pornography, false religion, gambling, etc.)

F)we must choose God over money

G)Jesus is the living Lord; Diana is dead

1)her temple disappeared for centuries

2)Jesus' Kingdom continues to grow

3)Mt 16:18; Mt 13:31-33

Paul Preaches & Raises the Dead (Acts 20:1-12)

1)Introduction (vs 1)
 A)after the riot in Ephesus, Paul encouraged in his disciples
 B)he then sets out for Macedonia (see map)
2)Paul ministers in Macedonia & Greece (vs 2-6)
 A)Paul ministers throughout Macedonia (many words)
 B)he visited churches he had planted earlier
 C)Paul then goes to Greece & serves there for 3 months
  --spent most of his time in Corinth & wrote Romans
 D)Paul's plans to sail to Syria are postponed by Jews plotting
  to kill him; Paul travels back through Macedonia
 E)Paul eventually travels to Troas (stays there one week)
 F)representatives from the churches accompany Paul
  1)Sopater of Berea
  2)Aristarchus & Secundus of Thessalonica
  3)Gaius of Derbe
  4)Timothy, Tychicus, & Trophimus of Asia
  5)these men went ahead of Paul & Luke ("us") &
   waited for them at Troas (reunited there)
 G)Acts records "true" history, not myths
  1)time—during the Feast of Unleavened Bread
  2)people—names of men (some now forgotten)
  3)places—the cities & regions where Paul traveled
3)Sunday Worship (vs 7)
 A)the Sabbath Day had been the Jewish day of worship (in
  memory of God's resting from His creation work)
 B)now, as early as 56AD, Christians worshiped on Sunday in
  celebration of Christ's resurrection
 C)1 Cor 16:1; Rev 1:10; Hb 4:7-10; Mt 11:28; Rm 14:1-5
4)Paul Preaches & Raises the Dead (vs 7-12)
 A)at Troas, the believers came together to celebrate the
  Lord's Supper on the first day of the week
 B)Paul was leaving the next day

C)Paul preached to them until midnight
D)many lamps in the upper room (very hot; very late)
E)a young man named Eutychus sat in a window
    1)he probably needed cool air to stay awake
    2)young man = neanias (about 8 to 14 years old)
    3)as Paul preached, he fell asleep
    4)Eutychus fell to his death from the 3rd story
    5)Paul embraced the corpse & raised him from the dead
    6)this comforted the believers
F)Paul celebrated the Lord's Supper with the Troas believers,
    ate with them, & continued teaching until daybreak
G)Paul apparently preached for 6 to 10 hours!
H)contemporary loss of respect for preaching of God's Word
    1)many of today's preachers are often:
        a)bi-vocational (no longer a respected profession)
        b)forced to be counselors or C.E.O.'s
    2)loss of respect for preaching (John Stott)
        a)anti-authority (desire for autonomy)
        b)modern technology & entertainment
            1)TV, computers, movies, concerts
            2)more visual, entertaining
            3)less attention span
        c)the church's loss of confidence in the Gospel
          --psychology, prosperity, secularism
        d)our desire to be flattered, not convicted
          --new age myths (2 Tm 4:1-5)
    3)if Paul were here today, would we permit him to
      speak for 6 to 10 hours?
    4)today, most Christians think 40 minutes is far too
      long a sermon (movies, sports events, concerts)

Paul's Farewell Sermon to the Ephesian Elders
(Acts 20:13-38)

1)<u>Introduction</u>—Paul travels to Miletus (vs 13-16)
    A)after leaving Troas, Paul eventually met his colleagues at
        Assos, en route to Miletus
    B)Paul rushed to reach Jerusalem for the Feast of Pentecost
    C)again, Luke records true history with specific details
2)<u>Paul sends for the Ephesian elders</u> (vs 17)
    A)he wishes to speak to them in Miletus
    B)it is the last time they will see each other
3)<u>Paul's farewell sermon to the Ephesian elders</u> (vs 18-35)
    A)<u>Paul reviews the past</u> (18-22)
        1)he had humbly served the Lord in Asia
        2)with tears & trials due to plots of the Jews
        3)Paul did not back down
        4)he taught the Ephesians
            a)publicly in synagogues & school of Tyrannus
            b)privately from house to house
        5)he witnessed to both Jews & Greeks
            a)repentance toward God (turn from sin &
                idolatry to God)
            b)faith in our Lord Jesus Christ (trust in Jesus
                alone for salvation; Jesus is God & Messiah)
    B)<u>Paul's plan to visit Jerusalem</u> (22-24)
        1)bound in the Spirit = led by the Holy Spirit
        2)Paul knows he will be persecuted in Jerusalem
        3)serving Jesus & finishing the race is more important
            to Paul than his physical well-being
        4)preaching the Gospel is more important than life
    C)<u>the Ephesian elders will never see Paul again</u> (25)
    D)<u>Paul is innocent of the blood of all men</u> (26-27)
        1)he proclaimed the whole truth of God
        2)he made the most of every opportunity& sounded the
            trumpet like a faithful watchman (Ezk 33:1-9)

E)Paul tells them to guard the flock (28-31)
    1)guard yourselves & the flock
    2)the Holy Spirit appointed them overseers over their
        flock—shepherd the church (assembly) of God
    3)shepherd (feed, protect, guide, love, etc.)
    4)God bought the church with His blood (Jesus is God)
    5)after Paul leaves, savage wolves will enter the church
        a)false prophets, false teachers
        b)wolves in sheep's clothing (Matthew 7:15)
    6)they will not spare the flock (deception)
    7)also, wolves from within (1 John 2:18-19)
    8)Jude 3-4; 2 Pt 2:1-3; Titus 1:9; 2 Tm 4:1-5;
        Eph 4:11-15; Rev 2:1-6
    9)false teachers distort the truth & gather disciples
    10)Paul earnestly warned them about this for 3 years
F)Paul commits the Ephesian elders to God (32)
    1)Paul will no longer be with them
    2)he entrusts them to God & His Word
    3)the Word builds our faith (Rm 10:17)
    4)only those who endure receive the inheritance
G)Paul did not covet their money (33-35)
    1)Paul earned his keep through tent-making
    2)Jesus' words, "It is more blessed to give then to
        receive." (not recorded in the 4 Gospels)
    3)Paul taught that preachers deserve their wages, but he
        didn't always exercise this right
    4)1 Tm 5:17-18; 1 Cor 9:9, 11-16
4)Paul prepares to leave (vs 36-38)
    A)Paul knelt & prayed with them all
    B)the elders wept & embraced Paul
    C)they were sad that they would not see him again
    D)they accompanied him to the ship

Paul Travels to Jerusalem Despites Warnings of Danger
(Acts 21:1-17)

1)Introduction

    A)Paul leaves Miletus where he had bid farewell to the Ephesian elders

    B)his plans to visit Jerusalem for the Feast of Pentecost (20:16, 22-24)

2)Paul departs for Jerusalem (vs 1-9) {refer to map}

    A)departed = after tearing ourselves away from them (Ephesian elders)

    B)set sail from Miletus to Cos (we = Luke was with Paul)

    C)the next day from Cos to Rhodes

    D)then from Rhodes to Patara (up to this point—smaller ships hugging the coast)

    E)then they took a larger ship & set sail for the region of Phoenicia

    F)they passed the Island of Cyprus & sailed to Syria, landing at Tyre

    G)they stayed with disciples in Tyre for seven days

    H)the disciples, through the Holy Spirit, warned Paul not to go to Jerusalem

    I)they prayed before sailing to Ptolemais

    J)at Ptolemais, Paul & his colleagues stayed with believers there for one day

    K)Paul & his colleagues then traveled to Caesarea & entered Philip's house

    L)Philip the evangelist was one of the seven deacons

        1)Acts 6:1-6; 8:1-13; 8:26-40

        2)he had four virgin daughters who prophesied (Matthew 19:10-12)

3)Agabus the Prophet Warns Paul of Danger in Jerusalem (vs 10-14)

    A)Paul & his colleagues stayed many days with Philip

    B)Agabus the Prophet came down to Caesarea from Judea

    C)probably the same one who prophesied the famine (11:27-30)

    D)he told Paul that the Jews at Jerusalem will bind Paul & turn him over to the

        Romans

    E)Paul's colleagues & the other disciples pleaded with him, trying to persuade

        him to not go to Jerusalem

F)but, Paul was convinced God had called him to go to Jerusalem despite any
                    persecution he would encounter there
        G)the disciples responded that the Lord's will be done
        H)the Holy Spirit was preparing Paul for the suffering he would experience, not
                    trying to get him to avoid the trip to Jerusalem (9:15)
4)Paul goes to Jerusalem (vs 15-17)
        A)Paul & his colleagues went to Jerusalem
        B)they were joined by some disciples from Caesarea (despite the danger)
        C)they brought with them Mnason of Cyprus
                1)an early disciple = one of the 70 or 120, or the first Pentecost?
                2)they lodged with him
        D)they came to Jerusalem & the believers gladly received them
5)Application—be willing to suffer for Jesus
        A)we must do God's will regardless of the costs
        B)Mark 10:28-31; John 15:18-20; 16:33 (Jesus said we would suffer persecution)
        C)2 Timothy 1:6-7; 3:12; 4:7, 18 (Paul said we would be persecuted)

Paul is Arrested in Jerusalem (Acts 21:17-40)

1)Introduction
  --Paul travels to Jerusalem despite the warnings; didn't look
  for trouble, but was always willing to suffer for Christ if necessary

2)The Jerusalem Christian leaders joyfully welcome Paul (vs 17-20)
  A)the brethren gladly received Paul & his colleagues
  B)Paul, Luke, & others meet with James and other leaders of the
    Jerusalem Church
  C)Paul gave a detailed summary of his work among the Gentiles
  D)the Jerusalem leaders glorified the Lord
  E)one true Church—both Jew & Gentile—Eph 2:11-18; Gal 3:26-29

3)The rumors circulating in Jerusalem about Paul (vs 20-22)
  A)Jerusalem believers were passionate about obeying the Law of
    Moses (symbolic, common ground, weaker brother, Judaizer)
  B)these believers were misled into thinking that Paul taught Jews to
    forsake circumcision and the Law of Moses
  C)criticism from fellow believers hurts most
  D)Paul's real position (1 Cor 9:19-22; Gal 2:1-3; Ac 16:1-4;
    Eph 2:8-9; Rm 3:20-23; 4:1-8; Gal 2:21)
  E)the Sanhedrin (the Jewish ruling Council) would probably meet
    once they learn that Paul is in Jerusalem

4)The Jerusalem Church leaders' plan for Paul (vs 23-26)
  A)four Jewish believers had taken a Nazarite vow (abstain from meat
    & wine, shave head, spend 7 days in temple courts, several
    sacrifices & offerings)
  B)Paul was advised to pay for the offerings & costs of these men to
    show he respects the Law of Moses
  C)this was consistent with Paul's own strategy (Rm 12:18; 1 Cor 9)
  D)the verdict of the Jerusalem Council 7 years earlier (vs 25; Ac 15)
  E)Paul agreed & tried to carry out the plan

5)Jews from Asia provoke the crowd against Paul (vs 27-30)
  A)probably from the Ephesus area; in Jerusalem for Pentecost
  B)they claimed Paul was anti-Law & that he brought a Gentile into
    the temple (the court of the Jews)

C)in reality, Paul did not bring Trophimus the Ephesian (Ac 20:4) into the court of the Jews (warning inscriptions found in 1871 & 1935—punishable by death)

D)the crowd dragged Paul out of the temple

E)immediately the doors of the temple were shut

6)A Roman commander protects Paul (vs 31-36)

A)the Antonia Fortress, rebuilt by Herod the Great, was connected to the outer court of the temple so that Roman soldiers could stifle Jewish riots

B)fellow Christians probably alerted the Romans of the riot

C)a commander supervised one-thousand men (centurion—100 men)

D)he arrested Paul both to protect him & to keep order

E)Paul was bound just as the Holy Spirit had revealed

F)"away with him!" (Lk 23:18; Jn 19:15)

7)Paul requests permission to address the angry crowd (vs 37-40)

A)the commander was surprised Paul spoke Greek

B)he thought Paul was a wanted Egyptian revolutionary (Josephus)

C)Paul told the commander who he was & asked for permission to speak to the angry mob

D)Paul startled the crowd by speaking to them in Hebrew (Aramaic)

8)Conclusion

A)there is only one true Church (all true believers from many nations)

B)salvation does not come through the works of the Law

C)salvation is by God's grace alone through faith alone in Jesus alone

D)the Law does not save (Gal 3:24; Rm 3:20-23)

E)try to be at peace with all men (Rm 12:18)

F)true believers will be persecuted & falsely accused (Jn 15:18)

G)Paul was willing to preach Jesus despite persecution

Paul Shares His Testimony with the Angry Jewish Mob
(Acts 22:1-30)

1)Introduction
    A)Paul arrested in Jerusalem due to angry Jewish mob
    B)Paul is allowed to speak to the crowd
    C)he speaks to them in Hebrew (Aramaic; Acts 21:40)

2)Paul shares his testimony (vs 1-21) {also found in Acts 9 & 26}
    A)he speaks about his Jewish background (1-5) {common ground}
        1)he spoke in Hebrew & tried to find common ground (1 Cor 9)
        2)I am a Jew (not a Gentile; 1 Cor 11:22; Php 3:4-6)
        3)born in Tarsus of Cilicia (a great university city of the ancient
            World—but Paul wasn't raised there)
        4)Paul was raised in Jerusalem
        5)he was discipled by Gamaliel—one of the greatest Jewish
            rabbis of his day (the School of Hillel; he died about 5
            years earlier)
        6)Paul was trained in the Mosaic Law (Gal 1:14)
        7)he had a passion for God (as did the crowd)
        8)Paul persecuted the Way (the church)
        9)he worked on behalf of the high priests & the Sanhedrin
        10)he traveled to Damascus to arrest Christians
    B)Jesus appeared to Paul on the road to Damascus (6-11)
        1)near Damascus Paul sees a great light from heaven
        2)Paul falls to the ground
        3)Jesus appears to him & asks why Paul is persecuting Him
        4)those with Paul saw the light but didn't hear the voice (they
            didn't hear with understanding)
        5)Acts 9:7—they heard the voice but couldn't make out what
            was said (they heard without understanding)
        6)Jesus told Paul to go to Damascus for further instructions
        7)Paul, blinded by the light, is led to Damascus
    C)A Christian named Ananias (12-16)
        1)Ananias was devout according to the Law (common ground-
            Paul did not come to destroy the Law-Mt 5:17-18)
        2)Ananias—a good reputation among Jews in Damascus
        3)he healed Paul & restored his sight

        4)the God of the Jewish Fathers had chosen Paul

        5)Paul would witness for Jesus to all men (Jew & Gentile)

        6)be baptized, wash away your sins, & call on the name of the
              Lord (baptism doesn't save—Rm 10:12-13)

    D)Paul returned to Jerusalem (17-21)

        1)three years later (Gal 1:18-19)

        2)Jesus appeared to Paul in the temple

        3)Jesus warned Paul to flee Jerusalem

        4)Jesus told him the Jews would reject his message

        5)Paul acknowledged he had persecuted Christians & his role in
              Stephen's martyrdom

        6)Jesus told Paul to leave Jerusalem & go to the Gentiles

3)The Crowd's Response (vs 22-23)

    A)they were surprised Paul spoke Hebrew/Aramaic

    B)probably impressed by Paul's training in the Law

    C)Paul's encounters with Jesus may have intrigued them

    D)however, they could not tolerate his statement about going to the
          Gentiles—they wanted to kill him

4)The Commander Intervenes (vs 24-30)

    A)he has Paul re-arrested & bound

    B)he didn't understand Paul's Hebrew speech

    C)he wanted Paul interrogated & scourged

    D)Paul tells the Romans that he is a Roman citizen by birth

    E)Roman citizens could not be scourged without a trial

    F)instead, the commander (fearing for his career) protects Paul &
          brings him before the Sanhedrin the next day

5)Conclusion—Sharing Our Testimony

    A)find common ground with our listeners (1 Cor 9)

    B)admit our sinfulness; don't exalt yourself (Rm 3:10, 23)

    C)exalt Jesus as Lord & Savior (Jn 14:6; Eph 2:8-9)

    D)provide evidence of a changed life & a new mission (2 Cor 5:17)

Paul on Trial Before the Sanhedrin (Acts 23:1-11)

1)Introduction
    A)the Holy Spirit warned Paul that persecution was ahead for him in Jerusalem; still, Paul went there
    B)a Jewish mob attempted to kill Paul
    C)Paul was placed under arrest by the Romans to protect him from the mob
    D)now he is on trial before the Jewish ruling council of 70 members

2)Paul on trial before the Sanhedrin (vs 1-10)
    A)Paul's exchange with the High Priest (vs 1-5)
        1)Paul looked earnestly at the council (vs 1)
            a)was he trying to see if he knew any of the members?
            b)about 25 years earlier (Acts 6:12)
        2)a good conscience before God
            a)Paul was not claiming to be perfect
            b)he always did what he thought God required
            c)he once thought God wanted Christians dead
            d)now he knows God wants the Gospel preached
            e)Paul always tried his best to obey God's laws
        3)Ananias the High Priest-ruled from 48 to 59 ad (vs 2)
            a)he ordered someone to strike Paul in the mouth
            b)he was known to be a man of bad character according to Josephus & the Jewish Talmud
            c)Jewish law protected defendants
        4)Paul protested to being hit (vs 3)
            a)God will strike you (God is the ultimate judge)
            b)you whitewashed wall—hypocrite (Mt 23:27)
            c)Paul is accused of being a law-breaker
            d)but in this case the judge is the law-breaker
            e)how Jesus responded (Jn 18:22-23; Mt 5:38-39)
        5)Paul is rebuked for speaking against the high priest (vs 5)
        6)Paul replies he did not know Ananias was the high priest
            a)Paul may have had poor sight (Gal 4:13-15; 6:11)
            b)Paul may not have known Ananias
            c)Ananias may not have been wearing his high priestly garments
            d)Paul admits he was wrong & quotes Ex 22:28
            e)this shows he knows & respects the Mosaic Law

B)<u>Paul divides the Sanhedrin</u> (vs 6-10)
      1)Paul saw that the Sanhedrin was almost evenly split between
          the Pharisees (rabbis) and the Sadducees (temple priests)
      2)Paul decided to divide his opposition—he knew he wasn't
          going to get a fair trial
      3)there was common ground he had with the Pharisees
      4)the Pharisees & the Christians both believed in the future
          bodily resurrection of God's true people
      5)Paul said, "I am a Pharisee" (present tense)
      6)Christianity is the fulfillment of Judaism, not its perversion
      7)Paul said his father was also a Pharisee
      8)Paul claimed he was on trial due to his belief in a future
        bodily resurrection (preaching Jesus' bodily resurrection
        points to the future resurrection of all God's people)
      9)this caused a division in the Sanhedrin between the Pharisees
          & the Sadducees
      10)Sadducees denied the resurrection, angels, & spirits (they
          only accepted the first 5 books of the Bible)
      11)the Pharisees believe in all three doctrines
      12)the Pharisees defended Paul—maybe an angel or a spirit
          spoke to him?
      13)there was so much confusion that the Roman commander
          ordered his soldiers to re-arrest Paul to protect him

3)<u>Jesus comforts & encourages Paul</u> (vs 11)
    A)Jesus appeared to Paul the following night
    B)Jesus comforted and encouraged Paul
    C)"be of Good cheer" (do not fear or be discouraged—Josh 1:9)
    D)"you have witnessed for me in Jerusalem"
    E)"you will also testify of me in Rome"
    F)Jesus let Paul know that he was in His will & that He would see to it
        that Paul preached the Gospel someday in Rome

4)<u>Conclusion</u>
    A)God's providence and sovereignty—God is in control
    B)despite the circumstance in which we find ourselves
    C)God protects His saints (Josh 1:9)
    D)preaching the Gospel is always the priority (Php 1:21)
    E)it is more important than our safety & well-being
    F)respect the governing authorities, even the evil ones (Rm 13:1)

Paul Rescued from Assassination Attempt (Acts 23:11-35)

1)Introduction
      A)Paul is imprisoned in Jerusalem
      B)Roman soldiers protect him from the angry Jewish leaders

2)Jesus Comforts & Encourages Paul (vs 11)
      A)Jesus appeared to Paul (Acts 9, 18, 22, 23)
      B)be encouraged, do not fear
      C)you preached about me in Jerusalem
      D)you will preach the Gospel in Rome
      E)no matter how bad things look, Jesus is still in control

3)The Plot to Assassinate Paul (vs 12-15)
      A)more than 40 men vowed not to eat or drink until they kill Paul
      B)they conspire with the leaders of the Sanhedrin (Sadducees mainly)
      C)John 16:2—killing Christians thought to be serving God

4)Paul's Nephew Exposes the Plot (vs 16-22)
      A)the son of Paul's sister hears of the plot
      B)he was a young man possibly in his 20's (neanias—Ac 7:58; 20:9)
      C)was he, like Paul before him, a Pharisee?

5)Paul is Transported to Caesarea (vs 23-24)
      A)the commander (leader of 1,000) sends 470 soldiers to transport
          Paul out of Jerusalem
      B)3rd hour of the night = 9pm

6)The Commander's Letter to Governor Felix (vs 25-30)
      A)the commander's name is Claudius Lysias
      B)he writes a letter to be taken to Governor Felix explaining Paul's
          situation (he does not mention he almost had Paul flogged)
      C)their law = Jewish theology, not Roman law
      D)Paul did not deserve death
      E)the Jews sought to kill him

7)Paul Confined in Caesarea (vs 31-35)
      A)the official Roman headquarters—not in Jerusalem, but in Caesarea
      B)Caesarea is 60 miles north of Jerusalem

C)Antipatris is 35 miles north of Jerusalem

D)all 470 soldiers escorted Paul to Antipatris

E)then, since they had left Jewish territory, only the 70 horsemen
accompanied Paul the rest of the way

F)the last 25 miles was flat & less vulnerable to an ambush

G)Felix = Governor of Judea from 52 to 60 ad

    1)a cruel man & former slave (Roman historian Tacitus)

    2)Suetonius wrote that Felix's 3 successive wives were all of
royal descent (1st wife was granddaughter of Antony &
Cleopatra; 3rd wife was Drusilla—the youngest daughter
of Herod Agrippa I)

    3)the political status of Cilicia did not require its citizens be
returned there for trial

    4)Felix would hear Paul's case when his accusers arrived

H)Herod's Praetorium = a palace built by Herod the Great; it had
prison cells

8)Conlusion

A)even the vilest of men (Ananias & Felix) cannot stifle the work of
God done through His people (Rm 8:31-33; Hb 13:5-6)

B)Jesus protected Paul from harm (Jn 16:33)

C)God is in control of our circumstances (Rm 8:28)

D)God must give His permission if believers are to be harmed (Job)

E)God protects faithful believers from death until our work is done;
then He takes us home (2 Tm 4:7; Dt 34:1-7)

F)Paul wrote many of his letters during & after this time (after 58 ad)

G)God was not finished using Paul

H)each new morning we arise—our work is not yet done
(Josh 1:9; Gal 6:9-10)

Paul on Trial Before Felix (Acts 24:1-27)

1)Introduction
  A)Paul is rescued from a plot to take his life
  B)he is taken to be tried by Governor Felix in Caesarea

2)The Charges Against Paul (vs 1-9)
  A)after 5 days (vs 1-4)
  B)Ananias the High Priest & the elders (i.e., leading members of the
      Sanhedrin) came to Caesarea to accuse Paul
  C)Tertullus, an orator, represented them
    1)trained in rhetoric (public speaking, debate)
    2)he acted as prosecuting attorney
  D)Tertullus attempted to flatter Felix
    1)he tried to win over Felix with lies
    2)Felix brought the Jews great peace & prosperity?
    3)through his foresight (his great wisdom)?
    4)the Jews were thankful for Felix's kind rule over them?
  E)Tertullus brings 3 charges against Paul (vs 5-6)
    1)political treason
        a)Paul caused dissension & riots among the Jews
            throughout the Roman Empire
        b)he is a ringleader of a sect—a revolutionary
        c)the death penalty for treason
    2)religious heresy
        a)a ringleader of the sect of the Nazarenes
        b)not really of the Jewish Faith
        c)no exemption from saying "Caesar is Lord"
    3)temple desecration
        a)they claimed he brought a Gentile into the Court of the
            Jews—Jews allowed to try temple criminals
        b)they claimed they wanted to try Paul in a civilized
            manner (Acts 21:27-29)
  F)Complaint against Commander Lysias (vs 7-9)
    1)by great violence he took Paul from the Jews
    2)Lysias was the cause of the violence, not the Jewish leaders
    3)now the case was brought before Felix

3)Paul's Defense: His Response to the Charges (vs 10-21)
    A)Paul knew that if he was convicted of treason he would be executed
    B)his response to the charge of treason
        1)he only went to Jerusalem 12 days earlier
        2)5 of the 12 days he was in Caesarea (24:1)
        3)impossible to start an insurrection against Rome in just 7 days
        4)he went to Jerusalem to worship, not to revolt
        5)he didn't cause a riot in the temple or anywhere else
    C)his response to the charges of religious heresy & temple desecration
        1)he did no wrong in the temple—he was there to worship
        2)though a follower of the Way (Jesus), he is still faithful to the
            Law of Moses (he still has the Jewish exemption)
        3)the Jews from Asia who accused him of bringing a Gentile
            into the Court of the Jews were not there to accuse him—
            the charges against him are hearsay
        4)he is faithful Jew—he brought donations for his nation
        5)he did no wrong at the Council
            a)his accusers before Felix were at the Council/Sanhedrin
            b)his only crime—he believed in the resurrection of the
                dead; but, only half the Council agreed with him

4)Felix Makes No Decision for 2 Years (vs 22-27)
    A)he knew the charges were fabricated—he had Paul treated well
    B)still, Felix wanted to please the Jews—he kept Paul in prison for 2
        Years; he hoped Paul would bribe him
    C)Felix had some knowledge of Christianity (his wife Drusilla was
        Herod Agrippa's daughter)
    D)Paul's messages of judgment terrified him—he was immoral
    E)Felix did the Jews a favor by keeping Paul in prison for 2 years—
        until Governor Festus replaced him
    F)Luke may have written Acts during these 2 years
    G)Felix was removed from being Governor around 60 ad when he
        used excessive force to quench a riot in Caesarea

5)Conclusion: Followers of Jesus:
    A)are obedient to the Old Testament Law (Jn 5:39-40; Lk 24:27)
    B)are good citizens—they do not cause riots (Rm 13:1-4; 12:18)
    C)often suffer for the sake of righteousness; they are often falsely
        accused (1 Pt 3:13-18; Jn 15:16-18)

Paul on Trial Before Festus: Paul Appeals to Caesar (Acts 25:1-12)

1)Festus replaces Felix as Governor
      A)Felix removed from office for using excessive force to stifle a riot
            in Caesarea; he was replaced by Festus
      B)apparently, Festus was an honest ruler

2)Festus visits Jerusalem (vs 1-5)
      A)a new governor often met with influential people in his region
      B)3 days after arriving in Caesarea, he went to Jerusalem to meet with
            the Chief Priests & other Sanhedrin leaders
      C)the Jewish leaders asked that Paul be brought to Jerusalem for trial
      D)again, they sought to kill Paul if he returned to Jerusalem
      E)Festus ruled that Paul would remain in Caesarea & be tried there

3)Paul on trial before Festus (vs 6-12)
      A)after 10 days in Jerusalem, Festus returned to Caesarea (the Jewish
            leaders also traveled to Caesarea)
      B)the Jews presented their charges against Paul
      C)however, they could not prove their charges
      D)Paul's defense—I have not broken the Law of the Jews, desecrated
            the Temple, or committed any offense against Rome
      E)Festus wanted to build a good relationship with the Jewish religious
            leaders—he asked if Paul were willing to be tried by the
            Sanhedrin in Jerusalem
      F)Paul's response:
            1)I'm already on trial in a Roman court
            2)I have not broken any Jewish Law
            3)I have committed no crime deserving death
            4)Paul knew he would be killed if he returned to Jerusalem
            5)the charges against Paul are unfounded
            6)I appeal my case to Caesar in Rome
      G)Festus, bound by Roman Law, allowed Paul to appeal his case to
            Rome

Paul Witnesses to King Agrippa (Acts 25:13-26:32)

1) Introduction
   - A) Paul was unjustly arrested in Jerusalem
   - B) he was taken to Caesarea for his safety
   - C) he was tried by Governors Felix & Festus
   - D) no guilt was found in Paul after over 2 years (Ac 24:27)
   - E) still, Paul appealed his case to Caesar

2) Festus gives King Agrippa the details of Paul's case (25:13-21)
   - A) Festus could not send Paul to Caesar without specifying the charges against Paul
   - B) Herod Agrippa II & his sister Bernice visited Festus to welcome him to his new position
     1) he was the son of Herod Agrippa I who died in 44 ad (Ac12)
     2) he ruled a portion of the Holy Land & had the right to appoint Jewish High Priests
     3) Herod Agrippa II had a greater knowledge about the Jewish religion than Festus did
     4) Festus took advantage of Herod's visit by telling him about Paul's case

3) Agrippa agrees to hear Paul's testimony (25:22-23)
   - A) Agrippa & Bernice entered accompanied by a great ceremony
   - B) Paul entered as a common man (Mt 19:30)

4) Festus asks Agrippa to help clarify the charges against Paul (25:24-27)

5) Paul shares his testimony with Agrippa (26:1-23)
   - A) Paul's early life (vs 1-11)
     1) Paul begins his speech by complimenting Agrippa (Mt 10:16)
     2) Paul relates that he was not a foreigner or a pagan
     3) he lived in Jerusalem & was trained as a Pharisee
        - a) Pharisees (rabbis, oral tradition, belief in resurrection)
        - b) Sadducees (temple priests, rejected resurrection)
     4) Paul views Jesus as the first fruits from the dead, the guarantee of the future resurrection of God's true children (1 Cor 15:20)
     5) Paul's faith is Jewish; he's not anti-temple or anti-Jewish
     6) still, originally Paul was opposed to Christ's followers
     7) he persecuted the Church with orders from the chief priests
     8) he hunted Christians from city to city

B)<u>Paul's conversion experience</u> (vs 12-18)

    1)Paul was on the road to Damascus, with orders from the chief priests, to arrest Christians

    2)a bright light from heaven knocked Paul & his colleagues to the ground

    3)Jesus appeared & spoke to Paul in Hebrew

        a)Saul, Saul, why are you persecuting Me?

        b)it is hard for you to kick against the goads (a stick with sharp end used to convince oxen to submit)

        c)Jesus was drawing Paul to Himself (Jn 12:32-33)

        d)Jesus would turn Paul into His witness

        e)to both Jews & Gentiles

            --to turn them from darkness to light (1 Jn 1:5-7)

            --from Satan's power to God (2 Cor 4:4)

        f)through faith in Jesus, one can receive forgiveness of sins & an eternal inheritance

C)<u>Paul's life after accepting Christ</u> (vs 19-23)

    1)Paul obeyed the heavenly vision—he is not a heretic

    2)he preached to Jew & Gentile that they should repent, turn to God, & do works consistent with repentance (metanoia)

    3)Paul's message is the same as that of Moses & the prophets

    4)Messiah would suffer, die, & be the first to rise/Ps 22; Isa 53

    5)Messiah would be a light to the Jews & the Gentiles/Isa 60

6)<u>Paul presses Agrippa to accept Christ</u> (26:24-29)

    A)Festus accuses Paul of being mad

    B)Paul says these things were not done in secret

    C)Paul asked Agrippa if he believed in the prophets

        1)if he said "no"—the Jews would reject Agrippa

        2)if he said "yes"—Agrippa would need to heed Paul's message

    D)Agrippa avoids Paul's question with his own question

        --do you really think you can convert me this quickly?

    E)Paul expresses love for Agrippa & the other listeners—he wishes they would all accept Christ & be like Paul, yet without chains

7)<u>Agrippa's opinion of Paul's case</u> (26:30-32)

    A)Paul was hard to refute & hard to dislike

    B)still, Agrippa knew there was no case against Paul

    C)Paul would have been set free had he not appealed to Caesar

8)<u>Conclusion</u>

    A)1 Peter 3:15 (always be ready to defend the faith, yet with
        gentleness & reverence)

    B)Colossians 4:5-6 (conduct yourself with wisdom towards
        non-believers)

    C)always be ready to share your testimony & defend the faith

    D)remind people you long to see them saved

Shipwrecked En Route to Rome: Lessons in Godly Leadership
(Acts 27:1-44)

1)Introduction
- A)Agrippa & Festus agree to send Paul to Rome to be tried by Caesar
- B)the Lord had appeared to Paul & told him he would testify of Jesus in Rome (Ac 23:11)
- C)Four of the most difficult times to lead:
  - 1)when you're not the official leader/prisoner
  - 2)when you're not considered an expert on the issue/tentmaker
  - 3)when the people aren't backing you
  - 4)during tough, disastrous times (shipwreck)

2)The Voyage from Caesarea to Sidon (vs 1-3)
- A)Julius—a centurion of the Augustan Regiment
  - 1)placed in charge of the prisoners
  - 2)he was kind & gracious to Paul
  - 3)he allowed Paul to visit his friends in Sidon
- B)Aristarchus—Paul's colleague & close friend
  - 1)a Macedonian from Thessalonica
  - 2)often by Paul's side (Ac 19:29; 20:4; Col 4:10; Phm 24)
- C)smaller ships would hug the coast during seasons of bad weather

3)The Voyage from Sidon to Myra (vs 4-6)
- A)hugging the coast for safety
- B)the prisoners were transferred to an Egyptian ship en route to Italy

4)The Voyage from Myra to Fair Havens (vs 7-12)
- A)the sailing was dangerous since the Day of Atonement was past
- B)that year, it fell in October when sailing became very difficult
- C)Paul warns the centurion not to continue the voyage (2 Cor 11:25)
- D)the season of fierce storms in the Mediterranean Sea had arrived
- E)the captain of the ship & the owner disagreed with Paul
- F)the centurion rejected Paul's warning & the voyage continued

5)The Voyage from Fair Havens to Malta (vs 13-44)
- A)Euroclydon = storm from the northeast (typhoon strength) {13-20}
- B)the ship was at the mercy of the wind; it could not sail against it
- C)cables used to under-gird the ship (to keep it together)
- D)they threw out all spare gear to lighten the ship

E)the storm kept the crew from seeing the stars or sky
F)there was no way for them to navigate
G)there appeared to be no hope of survival
H)long abstinence from food (nausea, fasting) {vs 21-26}
I)Paul's word of encouragement
      1)you should have listened to me earlier
      2)be courageous; no one will die
      3)an angel of God had appeared to Paul
      4)Paul will reach Rome; none will die
      5)the ship will run aground on an island
J)sailors attempted to escape {vs 27-32}
      1)Paul told the centurion
      2)the soldiers cut away the ropes of the lifeboat
      3)now, the centurion was following Paul's advice
K)Paul encourages the crew to eat—they will need strength {33-38}
      1)he told them they would all survive
      2)he thanked God for the bread in the sight of all
      3)he was calm & encouraging in the midst of the storm
      4)there were 276 people on board the ship
      5)after eating, they threw the rest of the grain overboard
L)the ship ran aground {39-44}
      1)the soldiers planned to kill the prisoners so that they could not
         escape (the soldiers would be responsible)
      2)but, the centurion respected Paul & wanted to spare his life
      3)he ordered his soldiers to refrain from killing the prisoners
      4)he ordered all to abandon ship & to swim to the shore
      5)just as Paul had predicted, all reached the shore safely

6)Lessons in Leadership
    A)a leader does not always have to appointed by man or an expert
    B)a leader does not always have to be popular
    C)a leader rises during disastrous times
    D)a leader remains calm in the midst of the storms of life
    E)a leader gives his people hope; he encourages them
    F)a leader motivates his people to do what must be done
    G)a leader unites the people to pursue a common goal
    H)a leader trusts God & His Word despite the circumstances
    I)a leader loves the people God has entrusted to him
    J)a leader views troubling circumstances as an opportunity to display
        leadership, an opportunity for God to act through him

Paul Arrives in Rome (Acts 28)

1)Introduction
> A)God promised Paul would witness in Rome (Ac 23:11)
> B)Paul was shipwrecked en route to Rome
> C)all were saved, but they were shipwrecked on an island

2)Paul on the Island of Malta (vs 1-10)
> A)Malta—60 miles to the south of Sicily
> B)Sicily was near the toe of Italy
> C)natives = barbaroi = barbarians (any people group that didn't speak
>> Greek (Rm 1:14)
> D)the natives were kind to Paul & the crew
> E)they made a fire to warm their visitors
> F)Paul gathered wood—not too important to do his share of work
>> 1)Booker T. Washington—college classes were full
>> 2)he accepted a job there making beds & sweeping floors until
>>> the next year when he could enroll—he excelled at his
>>> job (went on to be one of greatest thinkers in history)
> G)a viper bit his hand
> H)the islanders thought he was a murderer being punished
> I)Paul suffered no harm
> J)now, they thought he was a god (Acts 14:8-13)
> K)Publius—the Roman official in charge of Malta
> L)his father lay sick with fever & dysentery
>> 1)possibly Malta fever (common in Mediterranean islands)
>> 2)has now been traced to Maltese goats' milk
>> 3)the fever could last 4 months to 3 years
>> 4)dysentery = a disease characterized by severe diarrhea with
>>> passage of mucus & blood; usually caused by infection
>>> (Webster's dictionary)
> M)Paul prayed, laid his hands on him, & healed him
> N)other sick islanders came to Paul & were healed

3)Paul sails to Rome (vs 11-16)
> A)the crew stayed on the island for the winter months (Nov, Dec, Jan)
> B)they set sail on an Alexandrian ship
>> 1)it had a figurehead of Castor & Pollux—the twin brothers
>> 2)mythological sons of Zeus & protectors of sailors

C)stayed 3 days at Syracuse

D)reached Rhegium, & Puteoli

E)Puteoli = the port of Rome (some Christians met Paul there)

F)Christians from Rome traveled 33 miles south to Three Inns to greet
     Paul (excited that the famous apostle was coming to Rome)

G)other Christians from Rome traveled 10 miles farther south to meet
     Paul at the Appii Forum (ancient way of greeting a dignitary)

H)3 years earlier Paul wrote Rm 15:24

I)the Lord's promise to Paul (Ac 23:11)

J)Paul thanked God for the fellowship & was encouraged

K)finally, Paul arrives in Rome (1 Thes 5:24)

L)the prisoners were handed over to the captain of the guard

M)Paul was allowed to live in his own rented quarters, guarded by a
     soldier, & he was allowed to receive visitors

4)the Jews of Rome visit Paul (vs 17-29) {vs 17-22}

    A)former Emperor Claudius had expelled Jews from Rome (Ac 18:2);
       now his decree had lapsed; many Jews had returned to Rome

    B)after 3 days in Rome, Paul called the Jewish leaders to meet with
       him (Paul preached to Jews first, then to Gentiles; Ac 18:4, 6)

    C)Paul tells them he was falsely accused

    D)the Jews tell him they received no word about Paul

    E)did Paul's enemies give up or were they afraid of upsetting Caesar?

    F)the Jews of Rome were not interested in Paul's legal battle—they
       wanted to hear about Christianity (a sect of Judaism)

    G)on another day, Paul preached the Good News of Jesus to them,
       from the Old Testament, for a full day {vs 23-24}

    H)some were persuaded; some did not believe

    I)Paul quoted what Isaiah predicted about the Jewish rejection of
      Messiah (Isaiah 6:9-10) {vs 25-29}

        1)they would not see, hear, or understand the Gospel

        2) the Gospel would go to the Gentiles

        3)Isa 42:1; 49:6; 65:1-2; Rm 11;11

    J)the Jews left Paul's presence, debating his words

5)Paul preaches under house arrest for 2 years (vs 30-31)

    A)during this time, Paul preached to visitors

B)he also wrote 4 of his letters (Eph, Php, Col, Philemon)

C)he preached the Kingdom of God (wherever God rules)

    1)present, spiritual stage (in hearts of believers; Rm 14:17)

    2)physical, future stage (on earth when Jesus returns; Rv 11:15)

D)he taught about the Lord Jesus Christ

    1)Lord = Jesus is God (Kurios = Yahweh)

    2)Jesus = Jesus was really human, really a man

    3)Christ = Jesus is the Jewish Messiah & Savior of the world

E)with all confidence (boldness = parresias; Eph 6:18-20)

F)without hindrance (the Roman authorities did not prohibit him from

        Preaching—Luke emphasizes this for Theophilus)

6)Paul's later life

A)Acts ends abruptly in 61 ad with Paul in Rome under house arrest

B)Luke completed the letter & sent it to Theophilus

C)not mentioned in Acts: deaths of Peter, Paul, James; Jewish war

        with Rome; temple destruction (no events after 61 ad)

D)Paul was eventually released (Philemon 22; Php 1:19-23, 25)

E)Paul wrote 1 & 2 Tm & Titus after the close of Acts

F)Titus 1:5—Paul ministered in Crete

G)he may have preached in Spain (Rm 15:24)

H)later, he was rearrested, condemned, & beheaded in Rome between

        64 & 67 ad (2 Tm 4:6-8, 18)

7)Conclusion

A)the Gospel had been preached throughout the ancient world

        (Ac 1:8) & Paul preached in Rome

B)the early church was becoming less Jewish & more Gentile

C)we should not forget our Jewish roots & Old Testament foundation

D)Paul set the example for us by fighting the fight of faith (2 Tm 4:7)